A TEXTBOOK OF THEOSOPHY

Charles Webster Leadbeater

First published 1912

First published 2016
Copyright © 2016 Aziloth Books

All Rights Reserved. No part of this publication may be reproduced, stored in a retrieval system or transmitted in any form or by any means, electronic, mechanical, photocopying, recording, scanning or otherwise, except under the terms of the Copyright Licensing Agency Ltd, 90 Tottenham Court Road, London, W1P 0LP, UK, without the permission in writing of the Publisher. Requests to the Publisher should be via email to:
info@azilothbooks.com

Every effort has been made to contact all copyright holders. The publisher will be glad to make good in future editions any errors or omissions brought to their attention.

This publication is designed to provide authoritative and accurate information in regard to the subject matter covered. It is sold on the understanding that the Publisher is not engaged in rendering professional services.

British Library Cataloguing in Publication Data
A catalogue record for this book is available from the British Library

ISBN-13: 978-1-911405-25-2

Illustrations
Front cover: *Seal of the Theosophical Society* (with abstract background)
Title page: *Lotus*, Pixabay/TusitaStudio

CONTENTS

Chapter I
WHAT THEOSOPHY IS   4

Chapter II
FROM THE ABSOLUTE TO MAN   8

Chapter III
THE FORMATION OF A SOLAR SYSTEM   13

Chapter IV
THE EVOLUTION OF LIFE   18

Chapter V
THE CONSTITUTION OF MAN   25

Chapter VI
AFTER DEATH   36

Chapter VII
REINCARNATION   53

Chapter VIII
THE PURPOSE OF LIFE   59

Chapter IX
THE PLANETARY CHAINS   66

Chapter X
THE RESULT OF THEOSOPHICAL STUDY   73

Chapter I
WHAT THEOSOPHY IS

"There is a school of philosophy still in existence of which modern culture has lost sight." In these words Mr. A. P. Sinnett began his book, *The Occult World*, the first popular exposition of Theosophy, published thirty years ago.[1] During the years that have passed since then, many thousands have learned wisdom in that school, yet to the majority its teachings are still unknown, and they can give only the vaguest of replies to the query, "What is Theosophy?"

Two books already exist which answer that question: Mr. Sinnett's *Esoteric Buddhism* and Dr. Besant's *The Ancient Wisdom*. I have no thought of entering into competition with those standard works; what I desire is to present a statement, as clear and simple as I can make it, which may be regarded as introductory to them.

We often speak of Theosophy as not in itself a religion, but the truth which lies behind all religions alike. That is so; yet, from another point of view, we may surely say that it is at once a philosophy, a religion and a science. It is a philosophy, because it puts plainly before us an explanation of the scheme of evolution of both the souls and the bodies contained in our solar system. It is a religion in so far as, having shown us the course of ordinary evolution, it also puts before us and advises a method of shortening that course, so that by conscious effort we may progress more directly towards the goal. It is a science, because it treats both these subjects as matters not of theological belief but of direct knowledge obtainable by study and investigation. It asserts that man has no need to trust to blind faith, because he has within him latent powers which, when aroused, enable him to see and examine for himself, and it proceeds to prove its case by showing how those powers may be awakened. It is itself a result of the awakening of such powers by men, for the teachings which it puts before us are founded upon direct observations made in the past, and rendered possible only by such development.

As a philosophy, it explains to us that the solar system is a carefully-ordered mechanism, a manifestation of a magnificent life, of which man is but a small part. Nevertheless, it takes up that small part which immediately concerns us, and treats it exhaustively under three heads – present, past and future.

It deals with the present by describing what man really is, as seen by means of developed faculties. It is customary to speak of man as having a soul. Theosophy, as the result of direct investigation, reverses that dictum, and states that man is a soul, and has a body – in fact several bodies, which are his vehicles and instruments in various worlds. These worlds are not separate in space; they are simultaneously present with us, here and now, and can be examined; they are the divisions of the material side of Nature – different degrees of density in the aggregation of matter, as will presently be explained in detail. Man has an existence in several of these, but is normally conscious only of the lowest, though sometimes in dreams, and trances he has glimpses of some of the others. What is called death is the laying aside of the vehicle belonging to this lowest world, but the soul or real man in a higher world is no more changed or affected by this than the physical man is changed or affected when he removes his overcoat. All this is a matter, not of speculation, but of observation and experiment.

Theosophy has much to tell us of the past history of man – of how in the course of evolution he has come to be what he now is. This also is a matter of observation, because of the fact that there exists an indelible record of all that has taken place – a sort of memory of Nature – by examining which the scenes of earlier evolution may be made to pass before the eyes of the investigator as though they were happening at this moment. By thus studying the past we learn that man is divine in origin and that he has a long evolution behind him – a double evolution, that of the life or soul within, and that of the outer form. We learn, too, that the life of man as a soul is of, what to us seems, enormous length, and that what we have been in the habit of calling his life is in reality only one day of his real existence. He has already lived through many such days, and has many more of them yet before him; and if we wish to understand the real life and its object, we must consider it in relation not only to this one day of it, which begins with birth and ends with death, but also to the days which have gone before and those which are yet to come.

Of those that are yet to come there is also much to be said, and on this subject, too, a great deal of definite information is available. Such information is obtainable, first, from men who have already passed much further along the road of evolution than we, and have consequently direct experience of it; and, secondly, from inferences drawn from the obvious direction of the steps which we see to have been previously taken. The goal of this particular cycle is in sight, though still far above us but it would seem that, even when that has been attained, an infinity of progress still lies before everyone who is willing to undertake it.

One of the most striking advantages of Theosophy is that the light which it brings to us at once solves many of our problems, clears away many difficulties, accounts for the apparent injustices of life, and in all directions brings order out of seeming chaos. Thus, while some of its teaching is based upon the observation of forces whose direct working is somewhat beyond the ken of the ordinary man of the world, if the latter will accept it as a hypothesis he will very soon come to see that it must be a correct one, because it, and it alone, furnishes a coherent and reasonable explanation of the drama of life which is being played before him.

The existence of Perfected Men, and the possibility of coming into touch with Them and being taught by Them, are prominent among the great new truths which Theosophy brings to the western world. Another of them is the stupendous fact that the world is not drifting blindly into anarchy, but that its progress is under the control of a perfectly organized Hierarchy, so that final failure even for the tiniest of its units is of all impossibilities the most impossible. A glimpse of the working of that Hierarchy inevitably engenders the desire to co-operate with it, to serve under it, in however humble a capacity, and some time in the far-distant future to be worthy to join the outer fringes of its ranks.

This brings us to that aspect of Theosophy which we have called religious. Those who come to know and to understand these things are dissatisfied with the slow æons of evolution; they yearn to become more immediately useful, and so they demand and obtain knowledge of the shorter but steeper Path. There is no possibility of escaping the amount of work that has to be done. It is like carrying a load up a mountain; whether one carries it straight up a steep path or more gradually by a road of gentle slope, precisely the same number of foot-pounds must be exerted. Therefore to do the same work in a small fraction of the time means determined effort. It can be done, however, for it has been done; and those who have done it agree that it far more than repays the trouble. The limitations of the various vehicles are thereby gradually transcended, and the liberated man becomes an intelligent co-worker in the mighty plan for the evolution of all beings.

In its capacity as a religion, too, Theosophy gives its followers a rule of life, based not on alleged commands delivered at some remote period of the past, but on plain common sense as indicated by observed facts. The attitude of the student of Theosophy towards the rules which it prescribes resembles rather that which we adopt to hygienic regulations than obedience to religious commandments. We may say, if we wish, that this thing or that is in accordance with the divine Will, for the divine Will is expressed in what we know as the laws of Nature. Because that Will wisely ordereth all things, to infringe its laws means to disturb the smooth working of the scheme, to hold back for a moment that fragment or tiny part of evolution, and consequently to bring discomfort upon ourselves and others. It is for that reason that the wise man avoids infringing them – not to escape the imaginary wrath of some offended deity.

But if from a certain point of view we may think of Theosophy as a religion, we must note two great points of difference between it and what is ordinarily called religion in the West. First, it neither demands belief from its followers, nor does it even speak of belief in the sense in which that word is usually employed. The student of occult science either *knows* a thing or suspends his judgment about it; there is no place in his scheme for blind faith. Naturally, beginners in the study cannot yet *know* for themselves, so they are asked to read the results of the various observations and to deal with them as probable hypotheses – provisionally to accept and act upon them, until such time as they can prove them for themselves.

Secondly, Theosophy never endeavours to convert any man from whatever religion he already holds. On the contrary, it explains his religion to him, and enables him to see in it deeper meanings than he has ever known before. It teaches him to understand it and live it better than he did, and in many cases it gives back to him, on a higher and more intelligent level, the faith in it which he had previously all but lost.

Theosophy has its aspects as a science also; it is in very truth a science of life, a science of the soul. It applies to everything the scientific method of oft-repeated, painstaking observation, and then tabulates the results and makes deductions from them. In this way it has investigated the various planes of Nature, the conditions of man's consciousness during life and after what is commonly called death. It cannot be too often repeated that its statements on all these matters are not vague guesses or tenets of faith, but are based upon direct and oft-repeated *observation* of what happens. Its investigators have dealt also to a certain extent with subjects more in the range of ordinary science, as may be seen by those who read the book on *Occult Chemistry*.

Thus we see that Theosophy combines within itself some of the characteristics of philosophy, religion and science. What, it might be asked, is its gospel for this weary world? What are the main points which emerge from its investigations? What are the great facts which it has to lay before humanity?

They have been well summed up under three main heads.

"There are three truths which are absolute, and which cannot be lost, but yet may remain silent for lack of speech.

"The soul of man is immortal and its future is the future of a thing whose growth and splendour has no limit.

"The principle which gives life dwells in us and without us, is undying and eternally beneficent, is not heard or seen or smelt, but is perceived by the man who desires perception.

"Each man is his own absolute lawgiver, the dispenser of glory or gloom to himself, the decreer of his life, his reward, his punishment.

"These truths, which are as great as is life itself, are as simple as the simplest mind of man."

Put shortly, and in the language of the man of the street, this means that God is good, that man is immortal, and that as we sow so we must reap. There is a definite scheme of things; it is under intelligent direction and works under immutable laws. Man has his place in this scheme and is living under these laws. If he understands them and co-operates with them, he will advance rapidly and will be happy; if he does not understand them – if, wittingly or unwittingly, he breaks them, he will delay his progress and be miserable. These are not theories, but proved facts. Let him who doubts read on, and he will see.

---

[1] *Namely in 1881.*

Chapter II
FROM THE ABSOLUTE TO MAN

Of the Absolute, the Infinite, the All-embracing, we can at our present stage know nothing, except that It is; we can say nothing that is not a limitation, and therefore inaccurate.

In It are innumerable universes; in each universe countless solar systems. Each solar system is the expression of a mighty Being, whom we call the Logos, the Word of God, the Solar Deity. He is to it all that men mean by God. He permeates it; there is nothing in it which is not He; it is the manifestation of Him in such matter as we can see. Yet He exists above it and outside it, living a stupendous life of His own among His Peers. As is said in an Eastern Scripture: "Having permeated this whole universe with one fragment of Myself I remain."

Of that higher life of His we can know nothing. But of the fragment of His life which energises His system we may know something in the lower levels of its manifestation. We may not see Him, but we may see His power at work. No one who is clairvoyant can be atheistic; the evidence is too tremendous.

Out of Himself He has called this mighty system into being. We who are in it are evolving fragments of His life, Sparks of His divine Fire; from Him we all have come; into Him we shall all return.

Many have asked why He has done this; why He has emanated from Himself all this system; why He has sent us forth to face the storms of life. We cannot know, nor is the question practical; suffice it that we are here, and we must do our best. Yet many philosophers have speculated on this point and many suggestions have been made. The most beautiful that I know is that of a Gnostic philosopher:

"God is Love, but Love itself cannot be perfect unless it has those upon whom it can be lavished and by whom it can be returned. Therefore He put forth of Himself into matter, and He limited His glory, in order that through this natural and slow process of evolution we might come into being; and we in turn according to His Will are to develop until we reach even His own level, and then the very love of God itself will become more perfect, because it will then be lavished on those, His own children, who will fully understand and return it, and so His great scheme will be realized and His Will, be done."

At what stupendous elevation His consciousness abides we know not, nor can we know its true nature as it shows itself there. But when He puts Himself down into such conditions as are within our reach, His manifestation is ever threefold, and so all religions have imaged Him as a Trinity. Three, yet fundamentally One; Three Persons (for person means a mask) yet one God, showing Himself in those Three Aspects. Three to us, looking at Them from below, because Their functions are different; one to Him, because He knows Them to be but facets of Himself.

All Three of these Aspects are concerned in the evolution of the solar system; all Three are also concerned in the evolution of man. This evolution is His Will; the method of it is His plan.

Next below this Solar Deity, yet also in some mysterious manner part of Him, come His seven Ministers, sometimes called the Planetary Spirits. Using an analogy drawn from the physiology of our own body, Their relation to Him is like that of the ganglia or the nerve centres to the brain. All evolution which comes forth from Him comes through one or other of Them.

Under Them in turn come vast hosts or orders of spiritual beings, whom we call angels or devas. We do not yet know all the functions which they fulfil in different parts of this wonderful scheme, but we find some of them intimately connected with the building of the system and the unfolding of life within it.

Here in our world there is a great Official who represents the Solar Deity and is in absolute control of all the evolution that takes place upon this planet. We may image Him as the true King of this world and under Him are ministers in charge of different departments. One of these departments is concerned with the evolution of the different races of humanity so that for each great race there is a Head who founds it, differentiates it from all others, and watches over its development. Another department is that of religion and education, and it is from this that all the greatest teachers of history have come – that all religions have been sent forth. The great Official at the head of this department either comes Himself or sends one of His pupils to found a new religion when He decides that one is needed.

Therefore all religions, at the time of their first presentation to the world, have contained a definite statement of the Truth, and in its fundamentals this Truth has been always the same. The presentations of it have varied because of differences in the races to whom it was offered. The conditions of civilization and the degree of evolution obtained by various races have made it desirable to present this one Truth in divers forms. But the inner Truth is always the same, and the source from which it comes is the same, even though the external phases may appear to be different and even contradictory. It is foolish for men to wrangle over the question of the superiority of one teacher or one form of teaching to another, for the teacher is always one sent by the Great Brotherhood of Adepts, and in all its important points, in its ethical and moral principles, the teaching has always been the same.

There is in the world a body or Truth which lies at the back of all these religions, and represents the facts of nature as far as they are at present known to man. In the outer world, because of their ignorance of this, people are always disputing and arguing about whether there is a God; whether man survives death; whether definite progress is possible for him, and what is his relation to the universe. These questions are ever present in the mind of man as soon as intelligence is awakened. They are not unanswerable, as is frequently supposed; the answers to them are within the reach of anyone who will make proper efforts to find them. The truth is obtainable, and the conditions of its attainment are possible of achievement by anyone who will make the effort.

In the earlier stages of the development of humanity the great Officials of the Hierarchy are provided from outside, from other and more highly evolved parts of the system, but as soon as men can be trained to the necessary level of power and wisdom these offices are held by them. In order to be fit to hold such an office a man must raise himself to a very high level, and must become what is called an Adept – a being of goodness, power and wisdom so great that He towers above the rest of humanity, for He has already attained the summit of ordinary human evolution; He has achieved that which the plan of the Deity marked out for Him to achieve during this age or dispensation. But His evolution later on continues beyond that level – continues to divinity.

A large number of men have attained the Adept level – men not of one nation, but of all the leading nations of the world – rare souls who with indomitable courage have stormed the fortresses of nature, and captured her innermost secrets, and so have truly earned the right to be called Adepts. Among Them there are many degrees and many lines of activity; but always some of Them remain within touch of our earth as members of this Hierarchy which has in charge the administration of the affairs of our world and of the spiritual evolution of our humanity.

This august body is often called the Great White Brotherhood, but its members are not a community all living together. Each of Them, to a large extent, draws Himself apart from the world, and They are in constant communication with one another and with Their Head; but Their knowledge of higher forces is so great that this is achieved without any necessity for meeting in the physical world. In many cases They continue to live each in His own country, and Their power remains unsuspected among those who live near Them. Any man who will may attract Their attention, but he can do it only by showing himself worthy of Their notice. None need fear that his efforts will pass unnoticed; such over-sight is impossible, for the man who is devoting himself to service such as this, stands out from the rest of humanity like a great flame in a dark night. A few of these great Adepts, who are thus working for the good of the world, are willing to take as apprentices those who have resolved to devote themselves utterly to the service of mankind; such Adepts are called Masters. One of these apprentices was Helena Petrovna Blavatsky – a great soul who was sent out to offer knowledge to the world. With Colonel Henry Steel Olcott she founded The Theosophical Society for the spread of this knowledge which she had to give. Among those who came into contact with her in those early days was Mr. A. P. Sinnett, the editor of *The Pioneer*, and his keen intellect at once grasped the magnitude and the importance of the teaching which she put before him. Although Madame Blavatsky herself had previously written *Isis Unveiled*, it had attracted but little attention, and it was Mr. Sinnett who first made the teaching really available for western readers in his two books, *The Occult World* and *Esoteric Buddhism*.

It was through these works that I myself first came to know their author, and afterwards Madame Blavatsky herself; from both of them I learned much. When I asked Madame Blavatsky how one could learn still more, how one could make definite progress along the Path which she pointed out to us, she told me of the possibility that other students might be accepted as apprentices by the great Masters, even as she herself had been accepted, and that the only way to gain such acceptance was to show oneself worthy of it by earnest and altruistic work. She told me that to reach that goal a man must be absolutely one-pointed in his determination; that no one who tried to serve both God and Mammon could ever hope to succeed. One of these Masters Himself had said: "In order to succeed, a pupil must leave his own world and come into ours."

This means that he must cease to be one of the majority who live for wealth and power, and must join the tiny minority who care nothing for such things, but live only in order to devote themselves selflessly to the good of the world. She warned us clearly that the way was difficult to tread, that we should be misunderstood and reviled by those who still lived in the world, and that we had nothing to look forward to but the hardest of hard work; and though the result was sure, no one could foretell how long it would take to arrive at it. Some of us accepted these conditions joyfully, and we have never for a moment regretted the decision.

After some years of work I had the privilege of coming into contact with these great Masters of the Wisdom; from Them I learnt many things – among others, how to verify for myself at first hand most of the teachings which They had given. So that, in this matter, I write of what I know, and what I have seen for myself. Certain points are mentioned in the teaching, for the verification of which powers are required far beyond anything which I have gained so far. Of them, I can say only that they are consistent with what I do know, and in many cases are necessary as hypotheses to account for what I have seen. They came to me, along with the rest of the Theosophical system, upon the authority of these mighty Teachers. Since then I have learnt to examine for myself by far the greater part of what I was told, and I have found the information given to me to be correct in every particular; therefore I am justified in assuming the probability that that other part, which as yet I cannot verify, will also prove to be correct when I arrive at its level.

To attain the honour of being accepted as an apprentice of one of the

Masters of the Wisdom is the object set before himself by every earnest Theosophical student.

But it means a determined effort. There have always been men who were willing to make the necessary effort, and therefore there have always been men who knew. The knowledge is so transcendent that when a man grasps it fully he becomes more than man and he passes beyond our ken.

But there are stages in the acquirement of this knowledge, and we may learn much if we will, from those who themselves are still in process of learning; for all human beings stand on one or other of the rungs of the ladder of evolution. The primitive stand at its foot; we who are civilized beings have already climbed part of the way. But though we can look back and see rungs of the ladder below us which we have already passed, we may also look up and see many rungs above us to which we have not yet attained. Just as men are standing even now on each of the rungs below us, so that we can see the stages by which man has mounted, so also are there men standing on each of the rungs above us, so that from studying them we may see how man shall mount in the future. Precisely because we see men on every step of this ladder, which leads up to a glory which as yet we have no words to express, we know that the ascent to that glory is possible for us. Those who stand high above us, so high that They seem to us as gods in Their marvellous knowledge and power, tell us that They stood not long since where we are standing now, and They indicate to us clearly the steps which lie between, which we also must tread if we would be as They.

Chapter III
THE FORMATION OF A SOLAR SYSTEM

The beginning of the universe (if ever it had a beginning) is beyond our ken. At the earliest point of history that we can reach, the two great opposites of spirit and matter, of life and form, are already in full activity. We find that the ordinary conception of matter needs a revision, for what are commonly called force and matter are in reality only two varieties of Spirit at different stages in evolution and the real matter or basis of everything lies in the background unperceived. A French scientist has recently said: "There is no matter; there are nothing but holes in the ether." This also agrees with the celebrated theory of Professor Osborne Reynolds. Occult investigation shows this to be the correct view, and in that way explains what Oriental sacred books mean when they say that matter is an illusion.

The ultimate root-matter as seen at our level is what scientists call the ether of space.[2] To every physical sense the space occupied by it appears empty, yet in reality this ether is far denser than anything of which we can conceive. Its density is defined by Professor Reynolds as being ten thousand times greater than that of water, and its mean pressure as seven hundred and fifty thousand tons to the square inch.

This substance is perceptible only to highly developed clairvoyant power. We must assume a time (though we have no direct knowledge on this point) when this substance filled all space. We must also suppose that some great Being (not the Deity of a solar system, but some Being almost infinitely higher than that) changed this condition of rest by pouring out His spirit or force into a certain section of this matter, a section of the size of a whole universe. This effect of the introduction of this force is as that of the blowing of a mighty breath; it has formed within this ether an incalculable number of tiny spherical bubbles,[3] and these bubbles are the ultimate atoms of which what we call matter is composed. They are not the atoms of the chemist, nor even the ultimate atoms of the physical world. They stand at a far higher level, and what are usually called atoms are composed of vast aggregations of these bubbles, as will be seen later.

When the Solar Deity begins to make His system, He finds ready to His hand this material – this infinite mass of tiny bubbles which can be built up into various kinds of matter as we know it. He commences by defining the limit of His field of activity, a vast sphere whose circumference is far larger than the orbit of the outermost of His future planets. Within the limit of that sphere He sets up a kind of gigantic vortex – a motion which sweeps together all the bubbles into a vast central mass, the material of the nebula that is to be.

Into this vast revolving sphere He sends forth successive impulses of force, gathering together the bubbles into ever more and more complex aggregations, and producing in this way seven gigantic interpenetrating worlds of matter of different degrees of density, all concentric and all occupying the same space.

Acting through His Third Aspect He sends forth into this stupendous sphere the first of these impulses. It sets up all through the sphere a vast number of tiny vortices, each of which draws into itself forty-nine bubbles, and arranges them in a certain shape. These little groupings of bubbles so formed are the atoms of the second of the interpenetrating worlds. The whole number of the bubbles is not used in this way, sufficient being left in the dissociated state to act as atoms for the first and highest of these worlds. In due time comes the second impulse, which seizes upon nearly all these forty-nine bubble-atoms (leaving only enough to provide atoms for the second world), draws them back into itself and then, throwing them out again, sets up among them vortices, each of which holds within itself 2,401 bubbles (49^2). These form the atoms of the third world. Again after a time comes a third impulse, which in the same way seizes upon nearly all these 2,401 bubble-atoms, draws them back again into their original form, and again throws them outward once more as the atoms of the fourth world – each atom containing this time 49^3 bubbles. This process is repeated until the sixth of these successive impulses has built the atom of the seventh or the lowest world – that atom containing 49^6 of the original bubbles.

This atom of the seventh world is the ultimate atom of the physical world – not any of the atoms of which chemists speak, but that ultimate out of which all their atoms are made. We have at this stage arrived at that condition of affairs in which the vast whirling sphere contains within itself seven types of matter, all one in essence, because all built of the same kind of bubbles, "but differing in their degree of density. All these types are freely intermingled, so that specimens of each type would be found in a small portion of the sphere taken at random in any part of it, with, however, a general tendency of the heavier atoms to gravitate more and more towards the centre.

The seventh impulse sent out from the Third Aspect of the Deity does not, as before, draw back the physical atoms which were last made into the original dissociated bubbles, but draws them together into certain aggregations, thus making a number of different kinds of what may be called proto-elements, and these again are joined together into the various forms which are known to science as chemical elements. The making of these extends over a long period of ages, and they are made in a certain definite order by the interaction of several forces, as is correctly indicated in Sir William Crookes's paper, *The Genesis of the Elements*. Indeed the process of their making is not even now concluded; uranium is the latest and heaviest element so far as we know, but others still more complicated may perhaps be produced in the future.

As ages rolled on the condensation increased, and presently the stage of a vast glowing nebula was reached. As it cooled, still rapidly rotating, it flattened into a huge disc and gradually broke up into rings surrounding a central body – an arrangement not unlike that which Saturn exhibits at the present day, though on a far larger scale. As the time drew near when the planets would be required for the purposes of evolution, the Deity set up somewhere in the thickness of each ring a subsidiary vortex into which a great deal of the matter of the ring was by degrees collected. The collisions of the gathered fragments caused a revival of the heat, and the resulting planet was for a long time a mass of glowing gas. Little by little it cooled once more, until it became fit to be the theatre of life such as ours. Thus were all the planets formed.

Almost all the matter of those interpenetrating worlds was by this time concentrated into the newly formed planets. Each of them was and is composed of all those different kinds of matter. The earth upon which we are now living is not merely a great ball of physical matter, built of the atoms of that lowest world, but has also attached to it an abundant supply of matter of the sixth, the fifth, the fourth and other worlds. It is well known to all students of science that particles of matter never actually touch one another, even in the hardest of substances. The spaces between them are always far greater in proportion than their own size – enormously greater. So there is ample room for all the other kinds of atoms of all those other worlds, not only to lie between the atoms of the denser matter, but to move quite freely among them and around them. Consequently, this globe upon which we live is not one world, but seven interpenetrating worlds, all occupying the same space, except that the finer types of matter extend further from the centre than does the denser matter.

We have given names to these interpenetrating worlds for convenience in speaking of them. No name is needed for the first, as man is not yet in direct connection with it; but when it is necessary to mention it, it may be called the divine world. The second is described as the monadic, because in it exist those Sparks of the divine Life which we call the human Monads; but neither of these can be touched by the highest clairvoyant investigations at present possible for us. The third sphere, whose atoms contain 2,401 bubbles, is called the spiritual world, because in it functions the highest Spirit in man as now constituted. The fourth is the intuitional world,[4] because from it come the highest intuitions. The fifth is the mental world, because from its matter is built the mind of man. The sixth is called the emotional or astral world, because the emotions of man cause undulations in its matter. (The name astral was given to it by mediæval alchemists, because its matter is starry or shining as compared to that of the denser world.) The seventh world, composed of the type of matter which we see all around us, is called the physical.

The matter of which all these interpenetrating worlds are built is essentially the same matter, but differently arranged and of different degrees of density. Therefore the rates at which these various types of matter normally vibrate differ also. They may be considered as a vast gamut of undulations consisting of many octaves. The physical matter uses a certain number of the lowest of these octaves, the astral matter another group of octaves just above that, the mental matter a still further group, and so on.

Not only has each of these worlds its own type of matter; it has also its own set of aggregations of that matter – its own substances. In each world we arrange these substances in seven classes according to the rate at which their molecules vibrate. Usually, but not invariably, the slower oscillation involves also a larger molecule – a molecule, that is, built up by a special arrangement of the smaller molecules of the next higher subdivision. The application of heat increases the size of the molecules and also quickens and amplifies their undulation, so that they cover more ground, and the object, as a whole expands, until the point is reached where the aggregation of molecules breaks up, and the latter passes from one condition to that next above it. In the matter of the physical world the seven subdivisions are represented by seven degrees of density of matter, to which, beginning from below upwards, we give the names solid, liquid, gaseous, etheric, superetheric, sub-atomic and atomic.

The atomic subdivision is one in which all forms are built by the compression into certain shapes of the physical atoms, without any previous collection of these atoms into blocks or molecules. Typifying the physical ultimate atom for the moment by a brick, any form in the atomic subdivision would be made by gathering together some of the bricks, and building them into a certain shape. In order to make matter for the next lower subdivision, a certain number of the bricks (atoms) would first be gathered together and cemented into small blocks of say four bricks each, five bricks each, six bricks or seven bricks; and then these blocks so made would be used as building stones. For the next subdivision several of the blocks of the second sub-division cemented together in certain shapes would form building-stones, and so on to the lowest.

To transfer any substance from the solid condition to the liquid (that is to say, to melt it) is to increase the vibration of its compound molecules until at last they are shaken apart into the simpler molecules of which they were built. This process can in all cases be repeated again and again until finally any and every physical substance can be reduced to the ultimate atoms of the physical world.

Each of these worlds has its inhabitants, whose senses are normally capable of responding to the undulations of their own world only. A man living (as we are all-doing) in the physical world sees, hears, feels, by vibrations connected with the physical matter around him. He is equally surrounded by the astral and mental and other worlds which are interpenetrating his own denser world, but of them he is normally unconscious, because his senses cannot respond to the oscillations of their matter, just as our physical eyes cannot see by the vibrations of ultra-violet light, although scientific experiments show that they exist, and there are other consciousnesses with differently-formed organs who *can* see by them. A being living in the astral world might be occupying the very same space as a being living in the physical world, yet each would be entirely unconscious of the other and would in no way impede the free movement of the other. The same is true of all other worlds. We are at this moment surrounded by these worlds of finer matter, as close to us as the world we see, and their inhabitants are passing through us and about us, but we are entirely unconscious of them.

Since our evolution is centred at present upon this globe which we call the earth, it is in connection with it only that we shall be speaking of these higher worlds, so in future when I use the term "astral world" I shall mean by it the astral part of our own globe only, and not (as heretofore) the astral part of the whole solar system. This astral part of our own world is also a globe, but of astral matter. It occupies the same place as the globe which we see, but its matter (being so much lighter) extends out into space on all sides of us further than does the atmosphere of the earth – a great deal further. It stretches to a little less than the mean distance of the moon, so that though the two physical globes, the earth and the moon, are nearly 240,000 miles apart, the astral globes of these two bodies touch one another when the moon is in perigee, but not when she is in apogee. I shall apply the term "mental world" to the still larger globe of mental matter in the midst of which our physical earth exists. When we come to the still higher globes we have spheres large enough to touch the corresponding spheres of other planets in the system, though their matter also is just as much about us here on the surface of the solid earth as that of the others. All these globes of finer matter are a part of us, and are all revolving round the sun with their visible part. The student will do well to accustom himself to think of our earth as the whole of this mass of interpenetrating worlds – not only the comparatively small physical ball in the centre of it.

---

[2] *This has been described in Occult Chemistry under the name of koilon.*
[3] *The bubbles are spoken of in The Secret Doctrine as the holes which Fohat digs in space.*
[4] *Previously called in Theosophical literature the buddhic plane.*

Chapter IV
THE EVOLUTION OF LIFE

All the impulses of life which I have described as building the interpenetrating worlds come forth from the Third Aspect of the Deity. Hence in the Christian scheme that Aspect is called "the Giver of Life", the Spirit who brooded over the face of the waters of space. In Theosophical literature these impulses are usually taken as a whole, and called the First Outpouring.

When the worlds had been prepared to this extent, and most of the chemical elements already existed, the Second Outpouring of life took place, and this came from the Second Aspect of the Deity. It brought with it the power of combination. In all the worlds it found existing what may be thought of as elements corresponding to those worlds. It proceeded to combine those elements into organisms which it then ensouled, and in this way it built up the seven kingdoms of Nature. Theosophy recognizes seven kingdoms, because it regards man as separate from the animal kingdom and it takes into account several stages of evolution which are unseen by the physical eye, and gives to them the mediæval name of "elemental kingdoms".

The divine Life pours itself into matter from above, and its whole course may be thought of in two stages – the gradual assumption of grosser and grosser matter, and then the gradual casting off again of the vehicles which have been assumed. The earliest level upon which its vehicles can be scientifically observed is the mental – the fifth counting from the finer to the grosser, the first on which there are separated globes. In practical study it is found convenient to divide this mental world into two parts, which we call the higher and the lower according to the degree of density of their matter. The higher consists of the three finer subdivisions of mental matter; the lower part of the other four.

When the outpouring reaches the higher mental world it draws together the ethereal elements there, combines them into what at that level correspond to substances and of these substances builds forms which it inhabits. We call this the first elemental kingdom.

After a long period of evolution through different forms at that level, the wave of life, which is all the time pressing steadily downwards, learns to identify itself so fully with those forms that, instead of occupying them and withdrawing from them periodically, it is able to hold them permanently and make them part of itself, so that now from that level it can proceed to the temporary occupation of forms at a still lower level. When it reaches this stage we call it the second elemental kingdom, the ensouling life of which resides upon the higher mental levels, while the vehicles through which it manifests are on the lower.

After another vast period of similar length, it is found that the downward pressure has caused this process to repeat itself; once more the life has identified itself with its forms, and has taken up its residence upon the lower mental levels, so that it is capable of ensouling bodies in the astral world. At this stage we call it the third elemental kingdom.

We speak of all these forms as finer or grosser relatively to one another, but all of them are almost infinitely finer than any with which we are acquainted in the physical world. Each of these three is a kingdom of Nature, as varied in the manifestations of its different forms of life as is the animal or vegetable kingdom which we know. After a long period spent in ensouling the forms of the third of these elemental kingdoms it identifies itself with them in turn, and so is able to ensoul the etheric part of the mineral kingdom, and becomes the life which vivifies that – for there is a life in the mineral kingdom just as much as in the vegetable or the animal, although it is in conditions where it cannot manifest so freely. In the course of the mineral evolution the downward pressure causes it to identify itself in the same way with the etheric matter of the physical world, and from that to ensoul the denser matter of such minerals as are perceptible to our senses.

In the mineral kingdom we include not only what are usually called minerals, but also liquids, gases and many etheric substances the existence of which is unknown to western science. All the matter of which we know anything is living matter, and the life which it contains is always evolving. When it has reached the central point of the mineral stage the downward pressure ceases, and is replaced by an upward tendency; the outbreathing has ceased and the indrawing has begun.

When mineral evolution is completed, the life has withdrawn itself again into the astral world, but bearing with it all the results obtained through its experiences in the physical. At this stage it ensouls vegetable forms, and begins to show itself much more clearly as what we commonly call life – plant-life of all kinds; and at a yet later stage of its development it leaves the vegetable kingdom and ensouls the animal kingdom. The attainment of this level is the sign that it has withdrawn itself still further, and is now working from the lower mental world. In order to work in physical matter from that mental world it must operate through the intervening astral matter; and that astral matter is now no longer part of the garment of the group-soul as a whole, but is the individual astral body of the animal concerned, as will be later explained.

In each of these kingdoms it not only passes a period of time which is to our ideas almost incredibly long, but it also goes through a definite course of evolution, beginning from the lower manifestations of that kingdom and ending with the highest. In the vegetable kingdom, for example, the life-force might commence its career by occupying grasses or mosses and end it by ensouling magnificent forest trees. In the animal kingdom it might commence with mosquitoes or with animalculæ, and might end with the finest specimens of the mammalia.

The whole process is one of steady evolution, from, lower forms to higher, from the simpler to the more complex. But what is evolving is not primarily the form, but the life within it. The forms also evolve and grow better as time passes; but this is in order that they may be appropriate vehicles for more and more advanced waves of life. When the life has reached the highest level possible in the animal kingdom, it may then pass on into the human kingdom, under conditions which will presently be explained.

The outpouring leaves one kingdom and passes to another, so that if we had to deal with only one wave of this outpouring we could have in existence only one kingdom at a time. But the Deity sends out a constant succession of these waves, so that at any given time we find a number of them simultaneously in operation. We ourselves represent one such wave; but we find evolving alongside us another wave which ensouls the animal kingdom – a wave which came out from the Deity one stage later than we did. We find also the vegetable kingdom, which represents a third wave, and the mineral kingdom, which represents a fourth; and occultists know of the existence all round us of three elemental kingdoms, which represent the fifth, sixth and seventh waves. All these, however, are successive ripples of the same great outpouring from the Second Aspect of the Deity.

We have here, then, a scheme of evolution in which the divine Life involves itself more and more deeply in matter, in order that through that matter it may receive vibrations which could not otherwise affect it – impacts from without, which by degrees arouse within it rates of undulation corresponding to their own, so that it learns to respond to them. Later on it learns of itself to generate these rates of undulation, and so becomes a being possessed of spiritual powers.

We may presume that when this outpouring of life originally came forth from the Deity, at some level altogether beyond our power of cognition, it may perhaps have been homogeneous; but when it first comes within practical cognizance, when it is itself in the intuitional world, but is ensouling bodies made of the matter of the higher mental world, it is already not one huge world-soul but many souls. Let us suppose a homogeneous outpouring, which may be considered as one vast soul, at one end of the scale; at the other, when humanity is reached, we find that one vast soul broken up into millions of the comparatively little souls of individual men. At any stage between these two extremes we find an intermediate condition, the immense world-soul already subdivided, but not to the utmost limit of possible subdivision.

Each man is a soul, but not each animal or each plant. Man, as a soul, can manifest through only one body at a time in the physical world, whereas one animal soul manifests simultaneously through a number of animal bodies, one plant soul through a number of separate plants. A lion, for example, is not a permanently separate entity in the same way as a man is. When the man dies – that is, when he as a soul lays aside his physical body – he remains himself exactly as he was before, an entity separate from all other entities. When the lion dies, that which has been the separate soul of him is poured back into the mass from which it came – a mass which is at the same time providing the souls for many other lions. To such a mass we give the name of "group-soul".

To such a group-soul is attached a considerable number of lion bodies – let us say a hundred. Each of those bodies while it lives has its hundredth part of the group-soul attached to it, and for the time being this is apparently quite separate, so that the lion is as much an individual during his physical life as the man; but he is not a permanent individual. When he dies the soul of him flows back into the group-soul to which it belongs, and that identical lion-soul cannot be separated again from the group.

A useful analogy may help comprehension. Imagine the group-soul to be represented by the water in a bucket, and the hundred lion bodies by a hundred tumblers. As each tumbler is dipped into the bucket it takes out from it a tumblerful of water (the separate soul). That water for the time being takes the shape of the vehicle which it fills, "and is temporarily separate from the water which remains in the bucket, and from the water in the other tumblers.

Now put into each of the hundred tumblers some kind of colouring matter or some kind of flavouring. That will represent the qualities developed by its experiences in the separate soul of the lion during its lifetime. Pour back the water from the tumbler into the bucket; that represents the death of the lion. The colouring matter or the flavouring will be distributed through the whole of the water in the bucket, but will be a much fainter colouring, a much less pronounced flavour when thus distributed than it was when confined in one tumbler. The qualities developed by the experience of one lion attached to that group-soul are therefore shared by the entire group-soul, but in a much lower degree.

We may take out another tumblerful of water from that bucket, but we can never again get exactly the same tumblerful after it has once been mingled with the rest. Every tumblerful taken from that bucket in the future will contain some traces of the colouring or flavouring put into each tumbler whose contents have been returned to the bucket. Just so the qualities developed by the experience of a single lion will become the common property of all lions who are in the future to be born from that group-soul, though in a lesser degree than that in which they existed in the individual lion who developed them.

That is the explanation of inherited instincts; that is why the duckling which has been hatched by a hen takes to the water instantly without needing to be shown how to swim; why the chicken just out of its shell will cower at the shadow of a hawk; why a bird which has been artificially hatched, and has never seen a nest, nevertheless knows how to make one, and makes it according to the traditions of its kind.

Lower down in the scale of animal life enormous numbers of bodies are attached to a single group-soul – countless millions, for example, in the case of some of the smaller insects; but as we rise in the animal kingdom the number of bodies attached to a single group-soul becomes smaller and smaller, and therefore the differences between individuals become greater.

Thus the group-souls gradually break up. Returning to the symbol of the bucket, as tumbler after tumbler of water is withdrawn from it, tinted with some sort of colouring matter and returned to it, the whole bucketful of water gradually becomes richer in colour. Suppose that by imperceptible degrees a kind of vertical film forms itself across the centre of the bucket, and gradually solidifies itself into a division, so that we have now a right half and a left half to the bucket, and each tumblerful of water which is taken out is returned always to the same section from which it came.

Then presently a difference will be set up, and the liquid in one half of the bucket will no longer be the same as that in the other. We have then practically two buckets, and when this stage is reached in a group-soul it splits into two, as a cell separates by fission. In this way, as the experience grows ever richer, the group-souls grow smaller but more numerous, until at the highest point we arrive at man with his single individual soul, which no longer returns into a group, but remains always separate.

One of the life-waves is vivifying the whole of a kingdom; but not every group-soul in that life-wave will pass through the whole of that kingdom from the bottom to the top. If in the vegetable kingdom a certain group-soul has ensouled forest trees, when it passes on into the animal kingdom it will omit all the lower stages – that is, it will never inhabit insects or reptiles, but will begin at once at the level of the lower mammalia. The insects and reptiles will be vivified by group-souls which have for some reason left the vegetable kingdom at a much lower level than the forest tree. In the same way the group-soul which has reached the highest levels of the animal kingdom will not individualize into primitive savages, but into men of somewhat higher type, the primitive savages being recruited from group-souls which have left the animal kingdom at a lower level.

Group-souls at any level or at all levels arrange themselves into seven great types, according to the Minister of the Deity through whom their life has poured forth. These types are clearly distinguishable in all the kingdoms, and the successive forms taken by any one of them form a connected series, so that animals, vegetables, minerals and the varieties of the elemental creatures may all be arranged into seven great groups, and the life coming along one of those lines will not diverge into any of the others.

No detailed list has yet been made of the animals, plants or minerals from this point of view; but it is certain that the life which is found ensouling a mineral of a particular type will never vivify a mineral of any other type than its own, though within that type it may vary. When it passes on to the vegetable and animal kingdoms it will inhabit vegetables and animals of that type and of no other; and when it eventually reaches humanity it will individualize into men of that type and of no other.

The method of individualization is the raising of the soul of a particular animal to a level so much higher than that attained by its group-soul that it can no longer return to the latter. This cannot be done with any animal, but only with those whose brain is developed to a certain level, and the method usually adopted to acquire such mental development is to bring the animal into close contact with man. Individualization, therefore, is possible only for domestic animals, and only for certain kinds even of those. At the head of each of the seven types stands one kind of domestic animal – the dog for one, the cat for another, the elephant for a third, the monkey for a fourth, and so on. The wild animals can all be arranged on seven lines leading up to the domestic animals; for example, the fox and the wolf are obviously on the same line with the dog, while the lion, the tiger and the leopard equally obviously lead up to the domestic cat; so that the group-soul animating a hundred lions mentioned some time ago might at a later stage of its evolution have divided into, let us say, five group-souls each animating twenty cats.

The life-wave spends a long period of time in each kingdom; we are now only a little past the middle of such an æon, and consequently the conditions are not favourable for the achievement of that individualization which normally comes only at the end of a period. Rare instances of such attainment may occasionally be observed on the part of some animal much in advance of the average. Close association with man is necessary to produce this result. The animal if kindly treated develops devoted affection for his human friend, and also unfolds his intellectual powers in trying to understand that friend and to anticipate his wishes. In addition to this, the emotions and the thoughts of the man act constantly upon those of the animal, and tend to raise him to a higher level both emotionally and intellectually. Under favourable circumstances this development may proceed so far as to raise the animal altogether out of touch with the group to which he belongs, so that his fragment of a group-soul becomes capable of responding to the outpouring which comes from the First Aspect of the Deity.

For this final outpouring is not like the others, a mighty outrush affecting thousands or millions simultaneously; it comes to each one individually as that one is ready to receive it. This outpouring has already descended as far as the intuitional world; but it comes no farther than that until this upward leap is made by the soul of the animal from below; but when that happens this Third Outpouring leaps down to meet it, and in the higher mental world is formed an ego, a permanent individuality – permanent, that is, until, far later in his evolution, the man transcends it and reaches back to the divine unity from which he came. To make this ego, the fragment of the group-soul (which has hitherto played the part always of ensouling force) becomes in its turn a vehicle, and is itself ensouled by that divine Spark which has fallen into it from on high. That Spark may be said to have been hovering in the monadic world over the group-soul through the whole of its previous evolution, unable to effect a junction with it until its corresponding fragment in the group-soul had developed sufficiently to permit it. It is this breaking away from the rest of the group-soul and developing a separate ego which marks the distinction between the highest animal and the lowest man.

Chapter V
THE CONSTITUTION OF MAN

Man is therefore in essence a Spark of the divine Fire, belonging to the monadic world.[5] To that Spark, dwelling all the time in that world, we give the name "Monad". For the purposes of human evolution the Monad manifests itself in lower worlds. When it descends one stage and enters the spiritual world, it shows itself there as the triple Spirit having itself three aspects (just as in worlds infinitely higher the Deity has His three Aspects). Of those three one remains always in that world, and we call that the Spirit in man.

The second aspect manifests itself in the intuitional world, and we speak of it as the Intuition in man. The third shows itself in the higher mental world, and we call it the Intelligence in man. These three aspects taken together constitute the ego which ensouls the fragment from the group-soul. Thus man as we know him, though in reality a Monad residing in the monadic world, shows himself as an ego in the higher mental world, manifesting these three aspects of himself (Spirit, Intuition and Intelligence) through that vehicle of higher mental matter which we name the causal body.

This ego is the man during the human stage of evolution; he is the nearest correspondence, in fact, to the ordinary unscientific conception of the soul. He lives unchanged (except for his growth) from the moment of individualization until humanity is transcended and merged into divinity. He is in no way affected by what we call birth and death; what we commonly consider as his life is only a day in his life. The body which we can see, the body which is born and dies, is a garment which he puts on for the purposes of a certain part of his evolution.

Nor is it the only body which he assumes. Before he, the ego in the higher mental world, can take a vehicle belonging to the physical world, he must make a connection with it through the lower mental and astral worlds. When he wishes to descend he draws around himself a veil of the matter of the lower mental world, which we call his mental body. This is the instrument by means of which he thinks all his concrete thoughts – abstract thought being a power of the ego himself in the higher mental world.

Next he draws round himself a veil of astral matter, which we call his astral body; and that is the instrument of his passions and emotions, and also (in conjunction with the lower part of his mental body) the instrument. of all such thought as is tinged by selfishness and personal feeling. Only after having assumed these intermediate vehicles can he come into touch with a baby physical body, and be born into the world which we know. He lives through what we call his life, gaining certain qualities as the result of its experiences; and at its end, when the physical body is worn out, he reverses the process of descent and lays aside one by one the temporary vehicles which he has assumed. The first to go is the physical body, and when that is dropped, his life is centred in the astral world and he lives in his astral body.

The length of his stay in that world depends upon the amount of passion and emotion which he has developed within himself in his physical life. If there is much of these, the astral body is strongly vitalized, and will persist for a long time; if there is but little, the astral body has less vitality, and he will soon be able to cast that vehicle aside in turn. When that is done he finds himself living in his mental body. The strength of that depends upon the nature of the thoughts to which he has habituated himself, and usually his stay at this level is a long one. At last it comes to an end, and he casts aside the mental body in turn, and is once more the ego in his own world.

Owing to lack of development, he is as yet but partially conscious in that world; the vibrations of its matter are too rapid to make any impression upon him, just as the ultra-violet rays are too rapid to make any impression upon our eyes. After a rest there, he feels the desire to descend to a level where the undulations are perceptible to him, in order that he may feel himself to be fully alive; so he repeats the process of descent into denser matter, and assumes once more a mental, an astral and a physical body. As his previous bodies have all disintegrated, each in its turn, these new vehicles are entirely distinct from them, and thus it happens that in his physical life he has no recollection whatever of other similar lives which have preceded it.

When functioning in this physical world he remembers by means of his mental body; but since that is a new one, assumed only for this birth, it naturally cannot contain the memory of previous births in which it had no part. The man himself, the ego, does remember them all when in his own world, and occasionally some partial recollection of them or influence from them filters through into his lower vehicles. He does not usually, in his physical life, remember the experiences of earlier lives, but he does manifest in physical life the qualities which those experiences have developed in him. Each man is therefore exactly what he has made himself during those past lives; if he has in them developed good qualities in himself, he possesses the good qualities now; if he neglected to train himself, and consequently left himself weak and of evil disposition, he finds himself precisely in that condition now. The qualities, good or evil, with which he is born are those which he has made for himself.

This development of the ego is the object of the whole process of materialization; he assumes those veils of matter precisely because through them he is able to receive vibrations to which he can respond, so that his latent faculties may thereby be unfolded. Though man descends from on high into these lower worlds, it is only through that descent that a full cognizance of the higher worlds is developed in him. Full consciousness in any given world involves the power to perceive and respond to all the undulations of that world;

therefore the ordinary man has not yet perfect consciousness at any level – not even in this physical world which he thinks he knows. It is possible for him to unfold his percipience in all these worlds, and it is by means of such developed consciousness that we observe all these facts which I am now describing.

The causal body is the permanent vehicle of the ego in the higher mental world. It consists of matter of the first, second and third subdivisions of that world. In ordinary people it is not yet fully active, only that matter which belongs to the third subdivision being vivified. As the ego unfolds his latent possibilities through the long course of his evolution, the higher matter is gradually brought into action, but it is only in the perfected man whom we call the Adept that it is developed to its fullest extent. Such matter can be discerned by clairvoyant sight, but only by a seer who knows how to use the sight of the ego. It is difficult to describe a causal body fully, because the senses belonging to its world are altogether different from and higher than ours at this level. Such memory of the appearance of a causal body as it is possible for a clairvoyant to bring into his physical brain represents it as ovoid, and as surrounding the physical body of the man, extending to a distance of about eighteen inches from the normal surface of that body. In the case of primitive man it resembles a bubble, and gives the impression of being empty. It is in reality filled with higher mental matter, but as this is not yet brought into activity it remains colourless and transparent. As advancement continues it is gradually stirred into alertness by vibrations which reach it from the lower bodies. This comes but slowly, because the activities of man in the earlier stages of his evolution are not of a character to obtain expression in matter so fine as that of the higher mental body; but when a man reaches the stage where he is capable either of abstract thought or of unselfish emotion the matter of the causal body is aroused into response.

When these rates of undulation are awakened within him they show themselves in his causal body as colours, so that instead of being a mere transparent bubble it gradually becomes a sphere filled with matter of the most lovely and delicate hues – an object beautiful beyond all conception. It is found by experience that these colours are significant. The vibration which denotes the power of unselfish affection shows itself as a pale rose-colour; that which indicates high intellectual power is yellow; that which expresses sympathy is green, while blue betokens devotional feeling, and a luminous lilac-blue typifies the higher spirituality. The same scheme of colour-significance applies to the bodies which are built of denser matter, but as we approach the physical world the hues are in every case by comparison grosser – not only less delicate but also less living.

In the course of evolution in the lower worlds man often introduces into his vehicles qualities which are undesirable and entirely inappropriate for his life as an ego – such, for example, as pride, irritability, sensuality. These, like the rest, are reducible to vibrations, but they are in all cases vibrations of the lower subdivisions of their respective worlds, and therefore they cannot reproduce themselves in the causal body, which is built exclusively of the matter of the three higher subdivisions of its world. For each section of the astral body acts strongly upon the corresponding section of the mental body, but only upon the corresponding section; it cannot influence any other part. So the causal body can be affected only by the three higher portions of the astral body; and the oscillations of those represent only good qualities. The practical effect of this is that the man can build into the ego (that is, into his true self) nothing but good qualities; the evil qualities which he develops are in their nature transitory and must be thrown aside as he advances, because he has no longer within him matter which can express them. The difference between the causal bodies of the savage and the saint is that the first is empty and colourless, while the second is full of brilliant, coruscating tints. As the man passes beyond even saint-hood and becomes a great spiritual power, his causal body increases in size, because it has so much more to express, and it also begins to pour out from itself in all directions powerful rays of living light. In one who has attained Adeptship this body is of enormous dimensions.

The mental body is built of matter of the four lower subdivisions of the mental world, and expresses the concrete thoughts of the man. Here also we find the same colour-scheme as in the causal body. The hues are somewhat less delicate, and we notice one or two additions. For example, a thought of pride shows itself as orange, while irritability is manifested by a brilliant scarlet. We may see here sometimes the bright brown of avarice, the grey-brown of selfishness, and the grey-green of deceit. Here also we perceive the possibility of a mixture of colours; the affection, the intellect, the devotion may "be tinged by selfishness, and in that case their distinctive colours are mingled with the brown of selfishness, and so we have an impure and muddy appearance. Although its particles are always in intensely rapid motion among themselves, this body has at the same time a kind of loose organization.

The size and shape of the mental body are determined by those of the causal vehicle. There are in it certain striations which divide it more or less irregularly into segments, each of these corresponding to a certain department of the physical brain, so that every type of thought should function through its duly assigned portion. The mental body is as yet so imperfectly developed in ordinary men that there are many in whom a great number of special departments are not yet in activity, and any attempt at thought belonging to those departments has to travel round through some inappropriate channel which happens to be fully open. The result is that thought on those subjects is for those people clumsy and uncomprehending. This is why some people have a head for mathematics and others are unable to add correctly – why some people instinctively understand, appreciate and enjoy music, while others do not know one tune from another.

All the matter of the mental body should be circulating freely, but sometimes a man allows his thought upon a certain subject to set and solidify, and then the circulation is impeded, and there is a congestion which presently hardens into a kind of wart on the mental body. Such a wart appears to us down here as a prejudice; and until it is absorbed and free circulation restored, it is impossible for the man to think truly or to see clearly with regard to that particular department of his mind, as the congestion checks the free passage of undulations both outward and inward.

When a man uses any part of his mental body it not only vibrates for the time more rapidly, but it also temporarily swells out and increases in size. If there is prolonged thought upon a subject this increase becomes permanent, and it is thus open to any man to increase the size of his mental body either along desirable or undesirable lines.

Good thoughts produce vibrations of the finer matter of the body, which by its specific gravity tends to float in the upper part of the ovoid; whereas bad thoughts, such as selfishness and avarice, are always oscillations of the grosser matter, which tends to gravitate towards the lower part of the ovoid. Consequently the ordinary man, who yields himself not infrequently to selfish thoughts of various kinds, usually expands the lower part of his mental body, and presents roughly the appearance of an egg with its larger end downwards. The man who has repressed those lower thoughts, and devoted himself to higher ones, tends to expand the upper part of his mental body, and therefore presents the appearance of an egg standing on its smaller end. From a study of the colours and striations of a man's mental body the clairvoyant can perceive his character and the progress he has made in his present life. From similar features of the causal body he can see what progress the ego has made since its original formation, when the man left the animal kingdom.

When a man thinks of any concrete object – a book, a house, a landscape – he builds a tiny image of the object in the matter of his mental body. This image floats in the upper part of that body, usually in front of the face of the man and at about the level of the eyes. It remains there as long as the man is contemplating the object, and usually for a little time afterwards, the length of time depending upon the intensity and the clearness of the thought. This form is quite objective, and can be seen by another person, if that other has developed the sight of his own mental body. If a man thinks of another, he creates a tiny portrait in just the same way. If his thought is merely contemplative and involves no feeling (such as affection or dislike) or desire (such as a wish to see the person) the thought does not usually perceptibly affect the man of whom he thinks. If coupled with the thought of the person there is a feeling, as for example of affection, another phenomenon occurs besides the forming of the image. The thought of affection takes a definite form, which it builds out of the matter of the thinker's mental body. Because of the emotion involved, it draws round it also matter of his astral body, and thus we have an astromental form which leaps out of the body in which it has been generated, and moves through space towards the object of the feeling of affection. If the thought is sufficiently strong, distance makes absolutely no difference to it; but the thought of an ordinary person is usually weak and diffused, and is therefore not effective outside a limited area.

When this thought-form reaches its object it discharges itself into his astral and mental bodies, communicating to them its own rate of vibration. Putting this in another way, a thought of love sent from one: person to another involves the actual transference of a certain amount both of force and of matter from the sender to the recipient, and its effect upon the recipient is to arouse the feeling of affection in him, and slightly but permanently to increase his power of loving. But such a thought also strengthens the power of affection in the thinker, and therefore it does good simultaneously to both.

Every thought builds a form; if the thought be directed to another person it travels to him; if it be distinctly selfish it remains in the immediate neighbourhood of the thinker; if it belongs to neither of these categories it floats for awhile in space and then slowly disintegrates. Every man therefore is leaving behind him wherever he goes a trail of thought forms; as we go along the street we are walking all the time amidst a sea of other men's thoughts. If a man leaves his mind blank for a time, these residual thoughts of others drift through it, making in most cases but little impression upon him. Sometimes one arrives which attracts his attention, so that his mind seizes upon it and makes it its own, strengthens it by the addition of its force, and then casts it out again to affect somebody else. A man, therefore, is not responsible for a thought which floats into his mind, because it may be not his, but someone else's; but he is responsible if he takes it up, dwells upon it and then sends it out strengthened.

Self-centred thought of any kind hangs about the thinker, and most men surround their mental bodies with a shell of such thoughts. Such a shell obscures the mental vision and facilitates the formation of prejudice.

Each thought-form is a temporary entity. It resembles a charged battery, awaiting an opportunity to discharge itself. Its tendency is always to reproduce its own rate of vibration in the mental body upon which it fastens itself, and so to arouse in it a like thought. If the person at whom it is aimed happens to be busy or already engaged in some definite train of thought, the particles of his mental body are already swinging at a certain determinate rate, and cannot for the moment be affected from without. In that case the thought-form bides its time, hanging about its object until he is sufficiently at rest to permit its entrance; then it discharges itself upon him, and in the act ceases to exist.

The self-centred thought behaves in exactly the same way with regard to its generator, and discharges itself upon him when opportunity offers. If it be an evil thought, he generally regards it as the suggestion of a tempting demon, whereas in truth he tempts himself. Usually each definite thought creates a new thought-form; but if a thought-form of the same nature is already hovering round the thinker, under certain circumstances a new thought on the same subject, instead of creating a new form, coalesces with and strengthens, the old one, so that by long brooding over the same subject a man may sometimes create a thought-form of tremendous power. If the thought be a wicked one, such a thought-form may become a veritable evil influence, lasting perhaps for many years, and having for a time all the appearance and powers of a real living entity.

All these which have been described are the ordinary unpremeditated thoughts of man. A man can make a thought-form intentionally, and aim it at another with the object of helping him. This is one of the lines of activity adopted by those who desire to serve humanity. A steady stream of powerful thought directed intelligently upon another person may be of the greatest assistance to him. A strong thought-form may be a real guardian angel, and protect its object from impurity, from irritability or from fear.

An interesting branch of the subject is the study of the various shapes and colours taken by thought-forms of different kinds. The colours indicate the nature of the thought, and are in agreement with those which we have already described as existing in the bodies. The shapes are of infinite variety, but are often in some way typical of the kind of thought which they express.

Every thought of definite character, such as a thought of affection or hatred, of devotion or suspicion, of anger or fear, of pride or "jealousy, not only creates a form but also radiates an undulation. The fact that each one of these thoughts is expressed by a certain colour indicates that the thought expresses itself as an oscillation of the matter of a certain part of the mental body. This rate of oscillation communicates itself to the surrounding mental matter precisely in the same way as the vibration of a bell communicates itself to the surrounding air.

This radiation travels out in all directions, and whenever it impinges upon another mental body in a passive or receptive condition it communicates to it something of its own vibration. This does not convey a definite complete idea, as does the thought-form, but it tends to produce a thought of the same character as itself. For example, if the thought be devotional its undulations will excite devotion, but the object of the worship may be different in the case of each person upon whose mental body they impinge. The thought-form, on the other hand, can reach only one person, but will convey to that person (if receptive) not only a general devotional feeling, but also a precise image of the Being for whom the adoration was originally felt.

Any person who habitually thinks pure, good and strong thoughts is utilizing for that purpose the higher part of his mental body – a part which is not used at all by the ordinary man, and is entirely undeveloped in him. Such an one is therefore a power for good in the world, and is being of great use to all those of his neighbours who are capable of any sort of response. For the vibration which he sends out tends to arouse a new and higher part of their mental bodies, and consequently to open before them altogether new fields of thought.

It may not be exactly the same thought as that sent out, but it is of the same nature. The undulations generated by a man thinking of Theosophy do not necessarily communicate Theosophical ideas to all those around him; but they do awaken in them more liberal and higher thought than that to which they have before been accustomed. On the other hand, the thought-forms generated under such circumstances, though more limited in their action than the radiation, are also more precise; they can affect only those who are to some extent open to them, but to them they will convey definite Theosophical ideas.

The colours of the astral body bear the same meaning as those of the higher vehicles, but are several octaves of colours below them, and much more nearly approaching to such hues as we see in the physical world. It is the vehicle of passion and emotion, and consequently it may exhibit additional colours, expressing man's less desirable feelings, which cannot show themselves at higher levels; for example, a lurid brownishred indicates the presence of sensuality, while black clouds show malice and hatred. A curious livid grey betokens the presence of fear, and a much darker grey, usually arranged in heavy rings around the ovoid, indicates a condition of depression. Irritability is shown by the presence of a number of small scarlet flecks in the astral body, each representing a small angry impulse. Jealousy is shown by a peculiar brownish-green, generally studded with the same scarlet flecks. The astral body is in size and shape like those just described, and in the ordinary man its outline is usually clearly marked; but in the case of primitive man it is often exceedingly irregular, and resembles a rolling cloud composed of all the more unpleasant colours.

When the astral body is comparatively quiet (it is never actually at rest) the colours which are to be seen ;in it indicate those emotions to which the man is most in the habit of yielding himself. When the man experiences a rush of any particular feeling, the rate of vibration which expresses that feeling dominates for a time the entire astral body. If, for example, it be devotion, the whole of his astral body is flushed with blue, and while the emotion remains at its strongest the normal colours do little more than modify the blue, or appear faintly through a veil of it; but presently the vehemence of the sentiment dies away, and the normal colours reassert themselves. But because of that spasm of emotion the part of the astral body which is normally blue has been increased in size. Thus a man who frequently feels high devotion soon comes to have a large area of the blue permanently existing in his astral body.

When the rush of devotional *feeling* comes over him, it is usually accompanied by *thoughts* of devotion. Although primarily formed in the mental body, these draw round themselves a large amount of astral matter as well, so that their action is in both worlds. In both worlds also is the radiation which was previously described, so that the devotional man is a centre of devotion, and will influence other people to share both his thoughts and his feelings. The same is true in the case of affection, anger, depression – and, indeed, of all other feelings.

The flood of emotion does not itself greatly affect the mental body, although for a time it may render it almost impossible for any activity from that mental body to come through into the physical brain. That is not because that body itself is affected, but because the astral body, which acts as a bridge between it and the physical brain, is vibrating so entirely at one rate as to be incapable of conveying any undulation which is not in harmony with that.

The permanent colours of the astral body react upon the mental. They produce in it their correspondences, several octaves higher, in the same manner as a musical note produces overtones. The mental body in its turn reacts upon the causal in the same way, and thus all the good qualities expressed in the lower vehicles by degrees establish themselves permanently in the ego. The evil qualities cannot do so, as the rates of vibrations which express them are impossible for the higher mental matter of which the causal body is constructed.

So far, we have described vehicles which are the expression of the ego in their respective worlds – vehicles, which he provides for himself; in the physical world we come to a vehicle which is provided for him by Nature under laws which will be later explained – which, though also in some sense an expression of him, is by no means a perfect manifestation. In ordinary life we see only a small part of this physical body – only that which is built of the solid and liquid subdivisions of physical matter. The body contains matter of all the seven subdivisions, and all of them play their part in its life and are of equal importance, to it.

We usually speak of the invisible part of the physical body as the etheric double; "double" because it exactly reproduces the size and shape of the part of the body that we can see, and "etheric" because it is built of that finer kind of matter by the vibrations of which light is conveyed to the retina of the eye. (This must not be confused with the true ether of space – that of which matter is the negation.) This invisible part of the physical body is of great importance to us, since it is the vehicle through which flow the streams of vitality which keep the body alive, and without it, as a bridge to convey undulations of thought and feeling from the astral to the visible denser physical matter, the ego could make no use of the cells of his brain.

The life of a physical body is one of perpetual change and in order that it shall live, it needs constantly to be supplied from three distinct sources. It must have food for its digestion, air for its breathing, and vitality for its absorption. This vitality is essentially a force, but when clothed in matter it appears to us as a definite element, which exists in all the worlds of which we have spoken. At the moment we are concerned with that manifestation of it which we find in the highest sub-division of the physical world. Just as the blood circulates through the veins, so does the vitality circulate along the nerves; and precisely as any abnormality in the flow of the blood at once affects the physical body, so does the slightest irregularity in the absorption or flow of the vitality affect this higher part of the physical, body.

Vitality is a force which comes originally from the sun. When an ultimate physical atom is charged with it, it draws round itself six other atoms, and makes itself into an etheric element. The original force of vitality is then subdivided into seven, each of the atoms carrying a separate charge. The element thus made is absorbed into the human body through the etheric part of the spleen. It is there split up into its component parts, which at once flow to the various parts of the body assigned to them. The spleen is one of the seven force centres in the etheric part of the physical body. In each of our vehicles seven such centres should be in activity, and when they are thus active they are visible to clairvoyant sight. They appear usually as shallow vortices, for they are the points at which the force from the higher bodies enters the lower. In the physical body these centres are: (1) at the base of the spine, (2) at the solar plexus, (3) at the spleen, (4) over the heart, (5) at the throat, (6) between the eyebrows, and (7) at the top of the head. There are other dormant centres, but their awakening is undesirable.

The shape of all the higher bodies as seen by the clairvoyant is ovoid, but the matter composing them is not equally distributed throughout the egg. In the midst of this ovoid is the physical body. The physical body strongly attracts astral matter, and in its turn the astral matter strongly attracts mental matter. There-fore by far the greater part of the matter of the astral body is gathered within the physical frame; and the same is true of the mental vehicle. If we see the astral body of a man in its own world, apart from the physical body we shall still perceive the astral matter aggregated in exactly the shape of the physical, although, as the matter is more fluidic in its nature, what we see is a body built of dense mist, in the midst of an ovoid of much finer mist. The same is true for the mental body. Therefore, if in the astral or the mental world we should meet an acquaintance, we should recognise him by his appearance just as instantly as in the physical world.

This, then, is the true constitution of man. In the first place he is a Monad, a Spark of the Divine. Of that Monad the ego is a partial expression, formed in order that he may enter evolution, and may return to the Monad with joy, bringing his sheaves with him in the shape of qualities developed by garnered experience. The ego in his turn puts down part of himself for the same purpose into lower worlds, and we call that part a personality, because the Latin word persona means a mask, and this personality is the mask which the ego puts upon himself when he manifests in worlds lower than his own. Just as the ego is a small part and an imperfect expression of the Monad, so is the personality a small part and an imperfect expression of the ego; so that what we usually think of as the man is only in truth a fragment of a fragment.

The personality wears three bodies or vehicles, the mental, the astral and the physical. While the man is what we call alive and awake on the physical earth he is limited by his physical body, for he uses the astral and mental bodies only as bridges to connect himself with his lowest vehicle. One of the limitations of the physical body is that it quickly becomes fatigued and needs periodical rest. Each night the man leaves it to sleep, and withdraws into his astral vehicle, which does not become fatigued, and therefore needs no sleep. During this sleep of the physical body the man is free to move about in the astral world; but the extent to which he does this depends upon his development. The primitive savage usually does not move more than a few miles away from his sleeping physical form – often not as much as that; and he has only the vaguest consciousness. The educated man is generally able to travel in his astral vehicle wherever he will, and has much more consciousness in the astral world, though he has not often the faculty of bringing into his waking life any memory of what he has seen and done while his physical body was asleep. Sometimes he does remember some incident which he has seen, some experience which he has had, and then he calls it a vivid dream. More often his recollections are hopelessly entangled with vague memories of waking life, and with impressions made from without upon the etheric part of his brain. Thus we arrive at the confused and often absurd dreams of ordinary life. The developed man becomes as fully conscious and active in the astral world as in the physical, and brings through into the latter full remembrance of what he has been doing in the former – that is, he has a continuous life without any loss of consciousness throughout the whole twenty-four hours, and thus throughout the whole of his physical life, and even through death itself.

[5] *The President has now decided upon a set of names for the planes, so for the future these will be used instead of those previously employed. A table of them is given below for reference.*

NEW NAMES	OLD NAMES
1. Divine World	Âdi Plane
2. Monadic World	Anupâdaka Plane
3. Spiritual World	Âtmic or Nirvânic Plane
4. Intuitional World	Buddhic Plane
5. Mental World	Mental Plane
6. Emotional or Astral World	Astral Plane
7. Physical World	Physical Plane

These will supersede the names given in Vol. II of The Inner Life.

Chapter VI
AFTER DEATH

Death is the laying aside of the physical body; but it makes no more difference to the ego than does the laying aside of an overcoat to the physical man. Having put off his physical body, the ego continues to live in his astral body until the force has become exhausted which has been generated by such emotions and passions as he has allowed himself to feel during earth-life. When that has happened, the second death takes place; the astral body also falls away from him, and he finds himself living in the mental body and in the lower mental world. In that condition he remains until the thought-forces generated during his physical and astral lives have worn themselves out; then he drops the third vehicle in its turn and remains once more an ego in his own world, inhabiting his causal body.

There is, then, no such thing as death as it is ordinarily understood. There is only a succession of stages in a continuous life – stages lived in the three worlds one after another. The apportionment of time between these three worlds varies much as man advances. The primitive man lives almost exclusively in the physical world, spending only a few years in the astral at the end of each of his physical lives. As he develops, the astral life becomes longer, and as intellect unfolds in him, and he becomes able to think, he begins to spend a little time in the mental world as well. The ordinary man of civilized races remains longer in the mental world than in the physical and astral; indeed, the more a man evolves the longer becomes his mental life and the shorter his life in the astral world.

The astral life is the result of all feelings which have in them the element of self. If they have been directly selfish, they bring him into conditions of great unpleasantness in the astral world; if, though tinged with thoughts of self, they have been good and kindly, they bring him a comparatively pleasant though still limited astral life. Such of his thoughts and feelings as have been entirely unselfish produce their results in his life in the mental world; therefore that life in the mental world cannot be other than blissful. The astral life, which the man has made for himself either miserable or comparatively joyous, corresponds to what Christians call purgatory; the lower mental life, which is always entirely happy, is what is called heaven.

Man makes for himself his own purgatory and heaven, and these are not planes, but states of consciousness. Hell does not exist; it is only a figment of the theological imagination; but a man who lives foolishly may make for himself a very unpleasant and long enduring purgatory. Neither purgatory nor heaven can ever be eternal, for a finite cause cannot produce an infinite result. The variations in individual cases are so wide that to give actual figures is somewhat misleading. If we take the average man of what is called the lower middle class, the typical specimen of which would be a small shopkeeper or shop-assistant, his average life in the astral world would be perhaps about forty years, and the life in the mental world about two hundred. The man of spirituality and culture, on the other hand, may have perhaps twenty years of life in the astral world and a thousand in the heaven life. One who is specially developed may reduce the astral life to a few days or hours and spend fifteen hundred years in heaven.

Not only does the length of these periods vary greatly, but the conditions in both worlds also differ widely. The matter of which all these bodies are built is not dead matter but living, and that fact has to be taken into consideration. The physical body is built up of cells, each of which is a tiny separate life animated by the Second Outpouring, which comes forth from the Second Aspect of the Deity. These cells are of varying kinds and fulfil various functions, and all these facts must be taken into account if the man wishes to understand the work of his physical body and to live a healthy life in it.

The same thing applies to the astral and mental bodies. In the cell-life which permeates them there is as yet nothing in the way of intelligence, but there is a strong instinct always pressing in the direction of what is for its development. The life animating the matter of which such bodies are built is upon the outward arc of evolution, moving downwards or outwards into matter, so that progress for it means to descend into denser forms of matter, and to learn to express itself through them. Unfoldment for the man is just the opposite of this; he has already sunk deeply into matter and is now rising out of that towards his source. There is consequently a constant conflict of interests between the man within and the life inhabiting the matter of his vehicles, inasmuch as its tendency is downward, while his is upward.

The matter of the astral body (or rather the life animating its molecules) desires for its evolution such undulations as it can get, of as many different kinds as possible, and as coarse as possible. The next step in its evolution will be to ensoul physical matter and become used to its still slower oscillations; and as a step on the way to that, it desires the grossest of the astral vibrations. It has not the intelligence definitely to plan for these; but its instinct helps it to discover how most easily to procure them.

The molecules of the astral body are constantly changing, as are those of the physical body, but nevertheless the life in the mass of those astral molecules has a sense, though a very vague sense, of itself as a whole – as a kind of temporary entity. It does not know that it is part of a man's astral body; it is quite incapable of understanding what a man is; but it realizes in a blind way that under its present conditions it receives many more waves, and much stronger ones, than it would receive if floating at large in the atmosphere. It would then only occasionally catch, as from a distance, the radiation of man's passions and emotions; now it is in the very heart of them, it can miss none, and it gets them at their strongest. Therefore it feels itself in a good position, and it makes an effort to retain that position. It finds itself in contact with something finer than itself – the matter of the man's mental body; and it comes to feel that if it can contrive to involve that finer something in its own undulations, they will be greatly intensified and prolonged.

Since astral matter is the vehicle of desire and mental matter is the vehicle of thought, this instinct, when translated into our language, means that if the astral body can induce us to think that we want what it wants, it is much more likely to get it. Thus it exercises a slow steady pressure upon the man – a kind of hunger on its side, but for him a temptation to what is coarse and undesirable. If he be a passionate man there is a gentle but ceaseless pressure in the direction of irritability; if he be a sensual man, an equally steady pressure in the direction of impurity.

A man who does not understand this usually makes one of two mistakes with regard to it: either he supposes it to be the prompting of his own nature, and therefore regards that nature as inherently evil, or he thinks of the pressure as coming from outside – as a temptation of an imaginary devil. The truth lies between the two. The pressure is natural, not to the man but to the vehicle which he is using; its desire is natural and right for it, but harmful to the man, and therefore it is necessary that he should resist it. If he does so resist, if he declines to yield himself to the feelings suggested to him, the particles within him which need those vibrations become apathetic for lack of nourishment, and eventually atrophy and fall out from his astral body, and are replaced by other particles, whose natural wave-rate is more nearly in accordance with that which the man habitually permits within his astral body.

This gives the reason for what are called promptings of the lower nature during life. If the man yields himself to them, such promptings grow stronger and stronger until at last he feels as though he could not resist them, and identifies himself with them – which is exactly what this curious half-life in the particles of the astral body wants him to do.

At the death of the physical body this vague astral consciousness is alarmed. It realizes that its existence as a separated mass is menaced, and it takes instinctive steps to defend itself and to maintain its position as long as possible. The matter of the astral body is far more fluidic than that of the physical, and this consciousness seizes upon its particles and disposes them so as to resist encroachment. It puts the grossest and densest upon the outside as a kind of shell, and arranges the others in concentric layers, so that the body as a whole may become as resistant to friction as its constitution permits, and may therefore retain its shape as long as possible.

For the man this produces various unpleasant effects. The physiology of the astral body is quite different from that of the physical; the latter acquires its information from without by means of certain organs which are specialized as the instruments of its senses, but the astral body has no separated senses in our meaning of the word. That which for the astral body corresponds to sight is the power of its molecules to respond to impacts from without, which come to them by means of similar molecules. For example, a man has within his astral body matter belonging to all the subdivisions of the astral world, and it is because of that that he is capable of "seeing" objects built of the matter of any of these subdivisions.

Supposing an astral object to be made of the matter of the second and third subdivisions mixed, a man living in the astral world could perceive that object only if on the surface of his astral body there were particles belonging to the second and third subdivisions of that world which were capable of receiving and recording the vibrations which that object set up. A man who from the arrangement of his body by the vague consciousness of which we have spoken, had on the outside of that vehicle only the denser matter of the lowest subdivision, could no more be conscious of the object which we have mentioned than we are ourselves conscious in the physical body of the gases which move about us in the atmosphere or of objects built exclusively of etheric matter.

During physical life the matter of the man's astral body is in constant motion, and its particles pass among one another much as do those of boiling water.

Consequently at any given moment it is practically certain that particles of all varieties will be represented on the surface of his astral body, and that therefore when he is using his astral body during sleep he will be able to "see" by its means any astral object which approaches him.

After death, if he has allowed the rearrangement to be made (as from ignorance, all ordinary persons do) his condition in this respect will be different. Having on the surface of his astral body only the lowest and grossest particles, he can receive impressions only from corresponding particles outside; so that instead of seeing the whole of the astral world about him, he will see only one-seventh of it, and that the densest and most impure. The vibrations of this heavier matter are the expressions only of objectionable feelings and emotions, and of the least refined class of astral entities. Therefore it emerges that a man in this condition can see only the undesirable inhabitants of the astral world, and can feel only its most unpleasant and vulgar influences.

He is surrounded by other men, whose astral bodies are probably of quite ordinary character; but since he can see and feel only that which is lowest and coarsest in them, they appear to him to be monsters of vice with no redeeming features. Even his friends seem not at all what they used to be, because he is now incapable of appreciating any of their better qualities. Under these circumstances it is little wonder that he considers the astral world a hell; yet the fault is in no way with the astral world, but with himself – first, for allowing within himself so much of that cruder type of matter, and, secondly, for letting that vague astral consciousness dominate him and dispose it in that particular way.

The man who has studied these matters declines absolutely to yield to the pressure during life or to permit the rearrangement after death, and consequently he retains his power of seeing the astral world as a whole, and not merely the cruder and baser part of it.

The astral world has many points in common with the physical; just like the physical, it presents different appearances to different people, and even to the same person at different periods of his career. It is the home of emotions and of lower thoughts; and emotions are much stronger in that world than in this. When a person is awake we cannot see that larger part of his emotion at all; its strength goes in setting in motion the gross physical matter of the brain. So if we see a man show affection here, what we can see is not the whole of his affection, but only such part of it as is left after all this other work has been done. Emotions therefore bulk far more largely in the astral life than in the physical. They in no way exclude higher thought if they are controlled, so in the astral world as in the physical a man may devote himself to study and to helping his fellows, or he may waste his time and drift about aimlessly.

The astral world extends nearly to the mean distance of the orbit of the moon; but though the whole of this realm is open to any of its inhabitants who have not permitted the redistribution of their matter, the great majority remain much nearer to the surface of the earth. The matter of the different subdivisions of that world interpenetrates with perfect freedom, but there is on the whole a general tendency for the denser matter to settle towards the centre. The conditions are much like those which obtain in a bucket of water which contains in suspension a number of kinds of matter of different degrees of density. Since the water is kept in perpetual motion, the different kinds of matter are diffused through it; but in spite of that, the densest matter is found in greatest quantity nearest to the bottom. So that though we must not at all think of the various subdivisions of the astral world as lying above one another as do the coats of an onion, it is nevertheless true that the average arrangement of the matter of those subdivisions partakes somewhat of that general character.

Astral matter interpenetrates physical matter precisely as though it were not there, but each subdivision of physical matter has a strong attraction for astral matter of the corresponding subdivision. Hence it arises that every physical body has its astral counterpart. If I have a glass of water standing upon a table, the glass and the table, being of physical matter in the solid state, are interpenetrated by astral matter of the lowest sub-division. The water in the glass, being liquid, is interpenetrated by what we may call astral liquid – that is, by astral matter of the sixth subdivision; whereas the air surrounding both, being physical matter in the gaseous condition, is entirely interpenetrated by astral-gaseous matter – that is, astral matter of the fifth sub-division.

But just as air, water, glass and table are alike interpenetrated all the time by the finer physical matter which we have called etheric, so are all the astral counterparts interpenetrated by the finer astral matter of the higher subdivisions which correspond to the etheric. But even the astral solid is less dense than the finest of the physical ethers.

The man who finds himself in the astral world after death, if he has not submitted to the rearrangement of the matter of his body, will notice but little difference from physical life. He can float about in any direction at will, but in actual fact he usually stays in the neighbourhood to which he is accustomed. He is still able to perceive his house, his room, his furniture, his relations, his friends. The living, when ignorant of the .higher worlds, suppose themselves to have "lost" those who have laid aside their physical bodies; but the dead are never for a moment under the impression that they have lost the living. Functioning as they are in the astral body, the dead can no longer see the physical bodies of those whom they have left behind; but they do see their astral bodies, and as those are exactly the same in outline as the physical, they are perfectly aware of the presence of their friends. They see each one surrounded by a faint ovoid of luminous mist, and if they happen to be observant, they may notice various other small changes in their surroundings; but it is at least quite clear to them that they have not gone away to some distant heaven or hell, but still remain in touch with the world which they know, although they see it at a somewhat different angle.

The dead man has the astral body of his living friend obviously before him, so he cannot think of him as lost; but while the friend is awake, the dead man will not be able to make any impression upon him, for the consciousness of the friend is then in the physical world, and his astral body is being used only as a bridge. The dead man cannot therefore communicate with his friend, nor can he read his friend's higher thoughts; but he will see by the change in colour in the astral body any emotion which that friend may feel, and with a little practice and observation he may easily learn to read all those thoughts of his friend which have in them anything of self or of desire.

When the friend falls asleep the whole position is changed. He is then also conscious in the astral world side by side with the dead man, and they can communicate in every respect as freely as they could during physical life. The emotions felt by the living react strongly upon the dead who love them. If the former give way to grief, the latter cannot but suffer severely.

The conditions of life after death are almost infinite in their variety, but they can be calculated without difficulty by any one who will take the trouble to understand the astral world and to consider the character of the person concerned. That character is not in the slightest degree changed by death; the man's thoughts, emotions and desires are exactly the same as before. He is in every way the same man, minus his physical body; and his happiness or misery depends upon the extent to which this loss of the physical body affects him.

If his longings have been such as need a physical body for their gratification, he is likely to suffer considerably. Such a craving manifests itself as a vibration in the astral body, and while we are still in this world most of its strength is employed in setting in motion the heavy physical particles. Desire is therefore a far greater force in the astral life than in the physical, and if the man has not been in the habit of controlling it, and if in this new life it cannot be satisfied, it may cause him great and long-continued trouble.

Take as an illustration the extreme case of a drunkard or a sensualist. Here we have a lust which has been strong enough during physical life to overpower reason, common sense and all the feelings of decency and of family affection. After death the man finds himself in the astral world feeling the appetite perhaps a hundred times more strongly, yet absolutely unable to satisfy it because he has lost the physical body. Such a life is a very real hell – the only hell there is; yet no one is punishing him; he is reaping the perfectly natural result of his own action. Gradually as time passes this force of desire wears out, but only at the cost of terrible suffering for the man, because to him every day seems as a thousand years. He has no measure of time such as we have in the physical world. He can measure it only by his sensations. From a distortion of this fact has come the blasphemous idea of eternal damnation.

Many other cases less extreme than this will readily suggest themselves, in which a hankering which cannot be fulfilled may prove itself a torture. A more ordinary case is that of a man who has no particular vices, such as drink or sensuality, but yet has been attached entirely to things of the physical world, and has lived a life devoted to business or to aimless social functions. For him the astral world is a place of weariness; the only thing for which he craves are no longer possible for him, for in the astral world there is no business to be done, and, though he may have as much companionship as he wishes, society is now for him a very different matter, because all the pretences upon which it is usually based in this world are no longer possible.

These cases, however, are only the few, and for most people the state after death is much happier than life upon earth. The first feeling of which the dead man is usually conscious is one of the most wonderful and delightful freedom. He has absolutely nothing to worry about, and no duties rest upon him, except those which he chooses to impose upon himself. For all but a very small minority, physical life is spent in doing what the man would much rather not do; but he has to do it in order to support himself or his wife and family. In the astral world no support is necessary; food is no longer needed, shelter is not required, since he is entirely unaffected by heat or cold; and each man by the mere exercise of his thought clothes himself as he wishes.

For the first time since early childhood the man is entirely free to spend the whole of his time in doing just exactly what he likes.

His capacity for every kind of enjoyment is greatly enhanced, if only that enjoyment does not need a physical body for its expression. If he loves the beauties of Nature, it is now within his power to travel with great rapidity and without fatigue over the whole world, to contemplate all its loveliest spots, and to explore its most secret recesses. If he delights in art, all the world's masterpieces are at his disposal. If he loves music, he can go where he will to hear it, and it will now mean much more to him than it has ever meant before; for though he can no longer hear the physical sounds, he can receive the whole effect of the music into himself in far fuller measure than in this lower world. If he is a student of science, he can not only visit the great scientific men of the world, and catch from them such thoughts and ideas as may be within his comprehension, but also he can undertake researches of his own into the science of this higher world, seeing much more of what he is doing than has ever before been possible to him. Best of all, he whose great delight in this world has been to help his fellow men will still find ample scope for his philanthropic efforts.

Men are no longer hungry, cold, or suffering from disease in this astral world; but there are vast numbers who, being ignorant, desire knowledge – who, being still in the grip of desire for earthly things, need the explanation which will turn their thought to higher levels – who have entangled themselves in a web of their own imaginings, and can be set free only by one who understands these new surroundings and can help them to distinguish the facts of the world from their own ignorant misrepresentation of them. All these can be helped by the man of intelligence and of kindly heart. Many men arrive in the astral world in utter ignorance of its conditions, not realizing at first that they are dead, and when they do realize it fearing the fate that may be in store for them, because of false and wicked theological teaching. All of these need the cheer and comfort which can only be given to them by a man of common sense who possesses some knowledge of the facts of Nature.

There is thus no lack of the most profitable occupation for any man whose interests during his physical life have been rational; nor is there any lack of companionship. Men whose tastes and pursuits are similar drift naturally together there just as they do here; and many realms of Nature, which during our physical life are concealed by the dense veil of matter, now lie open for the detailed study of those who care to examine them.

To a large extent people make their own surroundings. We have already referred to the seven subdivisions of this astral world. Numbering these from the highest and least material downwards, we find that they fall naturally into three classes – divisions one, two and three forming one such class, and four, five and six another; while the seventh and lowest of all stands alone. As I have said, although they all interpenetrate, their substance has a general tendency to arrange itself according to its specific gravity, so that most of the matter belonging to the higher subdivisions is found at a greater elevation above the surface of the earth than the bulk of the matter of the lower portions.

Hence, although any person inhabiting the astral world can move into any part of it, his natural tendency is to float at the level which corresponds with the specific gravity of the heaviest matter in his astral body. The man who has not permitted the rearrangement of the matter of his astral body after death is entirely free of the whole astral world; but the majority, who do permit it, are not equally free – not because there is anything to prevent them from rising to the highest level or sinking to the lowest, but because they are able to sense clearly only a certain part of that world.

I have described something of the fate of a man who is on the lowest level, shut in by a strong shell of coarse matter. Because of the extreme comparative density of that matter he is conscious of less outside of his own subdivision than a man at any other level. The general specific gravity of his own astral body tends to make him float below the surface of the earth. The physical matter of the earth is absolutely non-existent to his astral senses, and his natural attraction is to that least delicate form of astral matter which is the counterpart of that solid earth. A man who has confined himself to that lowest subdivision will therefore usually find himself floating in darkness and cut off to a great extent from others of the dead, whose lives have been such as to keep them on a higher level.

Divisions four, five and six of the astral world (to which most people are attracted) have for their background the astral counterpart of the physical world in which we live, and all its familiar accessories. Life in the sixth subdivision is simply like our ordinary life on this earth minus the physical body and its necessities while as it ascends through the fifth and fourth divisions it becomes less and less material and is more and more withdrawn from our lower world and its interests.

The first, second and third sections, though occupying the same space, yet give the impression of being much further removed from the physical, and correspondingly less material. Men who inhabit these levels lose sight of the earth and its belongings; they are usually deeply self-absorbed, and to a large extent create their own surroundings, though these are sufficiently objective to be perceptible to other men of their level, and also to clairvoyant vision.

This region is the summerland of which we hear in spiritualistic circles – the world in which, by the exercise of their thought, the dead call into temporary existence their houses and schools and cities. These surroundings, though fanciful from our point of view, are to the dead as real as houses, temples or churches built of stone are to us, and many people live very contentedly there for a number of years in the midst of all these thought-creations.

Some of the scenery thus produced is very beautiful; it includes lovely lakes, magnificent mountains, pleasant flower gardens, decidedly superior to anything in the physical world; though on the other hand it also contains much which to the trained clairvoyant (who has learned to see things as they are) appears ridiculous – as, for example, the endeavours of the unlearned to make a thought-form of some of the curious symbolic descriptions contained in their various scriptures. An ignorant peasant's thought-image of a beast full of eyes within, or of a sea of glass mingled with fire, is naturally often grotesque, although to its maker it is perfectly satisfactory. This astral world is full of thought-created figures and landscapes. Men of all religions image here their deities and their respective conceptions of paradise, and enjoy themselves greatly among these dream-forms until they pass into the mental world and come into touch with something nearer to reality.

Everyone after death – any ordinary person, that is, in whose case the rearrangement of the matter of the astral body has been made – has to pass through all these subdivisions in turn. It does not follow that every one is conscious in all of them. The ordinarily decent person has in his astral body but little of the matter of its lowest portion – by no means enough to construct a heavy shell. The redistribution puts on the outside of the body its densest matter; in the ordinary man this is usually matter of the sixth subdivision, mixed with a little of the seventh, and so he finds himself viewing the counterpart of the physical world.

The ego is steadily withdrawing into himself, and as he withdraws he leaves behind him level after level of this astral matter. So the length of the man's detention in any section of the astral world is precisely in proportion to the amount of its matter which is found in his astral body, and that in turn depends upon the life he has lived, the desires he has indulged, and the class of matter which by so doing he has attracted towards him and built into himself. Finding himself then in the sixth section, still hovering about the places and persons with which he was most closely connected while on earth, the average man, as time passes on, finds the earthly surroundings gradually growing dimmer and becoming of less and less importance to him, and he tends more and more to mould his entourage into agreement with the more persistent of his thoughts. By the time that he reaches the third level he finds that this characteristic has entirely superseded the vision of the realities of the astral world.

The second subdivision is a shade less material than the third, for if the latter is the summerland of the spiritualists, the former is the material heaven of the more ignorantly orthodox; while the first or highest level appears to be the special home of those who during life have devoted themselves to materialistic but intellectual pursuits, following them not for the sake of benefiting their fellow men, but either from motives of selfish ambition or simply for the sake of intellectual exercise. All these people are perfectly happy. Later on they will reach a stage when they can appreciate something much higher, and when that stage comes they will find the higher ready for them.

In this astral life people of the same nation and of the same interest tend to keep together, precisely as they do here. The religious people, for example, who imagine for themselves a material heaven, do not at all interfere with men of other faiths whose ideas of celestial joy are different. There is nothing to prevent a Christian from drifting into the heaven of the Hindu or the Muhammadan, but he is little likely to do so, because his interests and attractions are all in the heaven of his own faith, along with friends who have shared that faith with him. This is by no means the true heaven described by any of the religions, but only a gross and material misrepresentation of it; the real thing will be found when we come to consider the mental world.

The dead man who has not permitted the rearrangement of the matter of his astral body is free of the entire world, and can wander all over it at will, seeing the whole of whatever he examines, instead of only a part of it as the others do. He does not find it inconveniently crowded, for the astral world is much larger than the surface of the physical earth, while its population is somewhat smaller, because the average life of humanity in the astral world is shorter than the average in the physical.

Not only the dead, however, are the inhabitants of this astral world, but always about one-third of the living as well, who have temporarily left their physical bodies behind them in sleep. The astral world has also a great number of non-human inhabitants, some of them far below the level of man, and some considerably above him. The nature-spirits form an enormous kingdom, some of whose members exist in the astral world, and make a large part of its population. This vast kingdom exists in the physical world also, for many of its orders wear etheric bodies and are only just beyond the range of ordinary physical sight. Indeed, circumstances not infrequently occur under which they can be seen, and in many lonely mountain districts these appearances are traditional among the peasants, by whom they are commonly spoken of as fairies, good people, pixies or brownies.

They are protean, but usually prefer to wear a miniature human form. Since they are not yet individualized, they may be thought of almost as etheric and astral animals; yet many of them are intellectually quite equal to average humanity. They have their nations and types just as we have, and they are often grouped into four great classes, and called the spirits of earth, water, fire and air. Only the members of the last of these four divisions normally confine their manifestation to the astral world, but their numbers are so prodigious that they are everywhere present in it.

Another great kingdom has its representatives here – the kingdom of the angels (called in India the devas). This is a body of beings who stand far higher in evolution than man, and only the lowest fringe of their hosts touches the astral world – a fringe whose constituent members are perhaps at about the level of development of what we should call a distinctly good man.

We are neither the only nor even the principal inhabitants of our solar system; there are other lines of evolution running parallel with our own which do not pass through humanity at all, though they must all pass through a level corresponding to that of humanity. On one of these other lines of evolution are the nature-spirits above described, and at a higher level of that line comes this great kingdom of the angels. At our present level of evolution they come into obvious contact with us only very rarely, but as we develop we shall be likely to see more of them – especially as the cyclic progress of the world is now bringing it more and more under the influence of the Seventh Ray. This Seventh Ray has ceremonial for one of its characteristics, and it is through ceremonial such as that of the Church or of Freemasonry that we come most easily into touch with the angelic kingdom.

When all the man's lower emotions have worn themselves out – all emotions, I mean, which have in them any thought of self – his life in the astral world is over, and the ego passes on into the mental world. This is not in any sense a movement in space; it is simply that the steady process of withdrawal has now passed beyond even the finest kind of astral matter; so that the man's consciousness is focussed in the mental world. His astral body has not entirely disintegrated, though it is in process of doing so, and he leaves behind him an astral corpse, just as at a previous stage of the withdrawal he left behind him a physical corpse. There is a certain difference between the two which should be noticed, because of the consequences which ensue from it.

When the man leaves his physical body his separation from it should be complete, and generally is so; but this is not the case with the much finer matter of the astral body. In the course of his physical life the ordinary man usually entangles himself so much in astral matter (which, from another point of view, means that he identifies himself so closely with his lower desires) that the indrawing force of the ego cannot entirely separate him from it again. Consequently, when he finally breaks away from the astral body and transfers his activities to the mental, he loses a little of himself, he leaves some of himself behind imprisoned in the matter of the astral body.

This gives a certain remnant of vitality to the astral corpse, so that it still moves freely in the astral world, and may easily be mistaken by the ignorant for the man himself – the more so as such fragmentary consciousness as still remains to it is part of the man, and therefore it naturally regards itself and speaks of itself as the man. It retains his memories, but is only a partial and unsatisfactory representation of him. Sometimes in spiritualistic seances one comes into contact with an entity of this description, and wonders how it is that one's friend has deteriorated so much since his death. To this fragmentary entity we give the name "shade".

At a later stage even this fragment of consciousness dies out of the astral body, but does not return to the ego to whom it originally belonged. Even then the astral corpse still remains, but when it is quite without any trace of its former life we call it a "shell". Of itself a shell cannot communicate at a seance, or take any action of any sort; but such shells are frequently seized upon by sportive nature-spirits and used as temporary habitations. A shell so occupied can communicate at a seance and masquerade as its original owner, since some of his characteristics and certain portions of his memory can be evoked by the nature-spirit from his astral corpse.

When a man falls asleep, he withdraws in his astral body, leaving the whole of the physical vehicle behind him. When he dies, he draws out with him the etheric part of the physical body, and consequently has usually at least a moment of unconsciousness while he is freeing himself from it. The etheric double is not a vehicle and cannot be used as such; so when the man is surrounded by it, he is for the moment able to function neither in the physical world nor the astral. Some men succeed in shaking themselves free of this etheric envelope in a few moments; others rest within it for hours, days or even weeks.

Nor is it certain that, when the man is free from this, he will at once become conscious of the astral world. For there is in him a good deal of the lowest kind of astral matter, so that a shell of this may be made around him. But he may be quite unable to use that matter.

If he has lived a reasonably decent life he is little in the habit of employing it or responding to its vibrations, and he cannot instantly acquire this habit. For that reason, he may remain unconscious until that matter gradually wears away, and some matter which he is in the habit of using comes on the surface. Such an occlusion, however, is scarcely ever complete, for even in the most carefully made shell some particles of the finer matter occasionally find their way to the surface, and give him fleeting glimpses of his surroundings.

There are some men who cling so desperately to their physical vehicles that they will not relax their hold upon the etheric double, but strive with all their might to retain it. They may be successful in doing so for a considerable time, but only at the cost of great discomfort to themselves. They are shut out from both worlds, and find themselves surrounded by a dense grey mist, through which they see very dimly the things of the physical world, but with all the colour gone from them. It is a terrible struggle for them to maintain their position in this miserable condition, and yet they will not relax their hold upon the etheric double, feeling that that is at least some sort of link with the only world that they know. Thus they drift about in a condition of loneliness and misery until from sheer fatigue their hold fails them, and they slip into the comparative happiness of astral life. Sometimes in their desperation they grasp blindly at other bodies, and try to enter into them, and occasionally they are successful in such an attempt. They may seize upon a baby body, ousting the feeble personality for whom it was intended, or sometimes they grasp even the body of an animal. All this trouble arises entirely from ignorance, and it can never happen to anyone who understands the laws of life and death.

When the astral life is over, the man dies to that world in turn, and awakens in the mental world. With him it is not at all what it is to the trained clairvoyant, who ranges through it and lives amidst the surroundings which he finds there, precisely as he would in the physical or astral worlds. The ordinary man has all through his life been encompassing himself with a mass of thought-forms. Some which are transitory, to which he pays little attention, have fallen away from him long ago, but those which represent the main interests of his life are always with him, and grow ever stronger and stronger. If some of these have been selfish, their force pours down into astral matter, and he has exhausted them during his life in the astral world. But those which are entirely unselfish belong purely to his mental body, and so when he finds himself in the mental world it is through these special thoughts that he is able to appreciate it.

His mental body is by no means fully developed; only those parts of it are really in action to their fullest extent which he has used in this altruistic manner. When he awakens again after the second death, his first sense is one of indescribable bliss and vitality – a feeling of such utter joy in living that he needs for the time nothing but just to live. Such bliss is of the essence of life in all the higher worlds of the system. Even astral life has possibilities of happiness far greater than anything that we can know in the dense body; but the heaven-life in the mental world is out of all proportion more blissful than the astral. In each higher world the same experience is repeated. Merely to live in any one of them seems the uttermost conceivable bliss; and yet, when the next one is reached, it is seen that it far surpasses the last.

Just as the bliss increases, so does the wisdom and the breadth of view. A man fusses about in the physical world and thinks himself so busy and so wise; but when he touches even the astral, he realizes at once that he has been all the time only a caterpillar crawling about and seeing nothing but his own leaf, whereas now he has spread his wings like the butterfly and flown away into the sunshine of a wider world. Yet, impossible as it may seem, the same experience is repeated when he passes into the mental world, for this life is in turn so much fuller and wider and more intense than the astral that once more no comparison is possible. And yet beyond all these there is still another life, that of the intuitional world, unto which even this is but as moon-light unto sunlight.

The man's position in the mental world differs widely from that in the astral. There he was using a body to which he was thoroughly accustomed, a body which he had been in the habit of employing every night during sleep. Here he finds himself living in a vehicle which he has never used before – a vehicle furthermore which is very far from being fully developed – a vehicle which shuts him out to a great extent from the world about him, instead of enabling him to see it. The lower part of his nature burnt itself away during his purgatorial life, and now there remain to him only his higher and more refined thoughts, the noble and unselfish aspirations which he poured out during earth-life. These cluster round him, and make a sort of shell about him, through the medium of which he is able to respond to certain types of vibrations in this refined matter.

These thoughts which surround him are the powers by which he draws upon the wealth of the heaven-world, and he finds it to be a storehouse of infinite extent, upon which he is able to draw just according to the power of those thoughts and aspirations; for in this world is existing the infinite fullness of the Divine Mind, open in all its limitless affluence to every soul, just in proportion as that soul has qualified itself to receive. A man who has already completed his human evolution, who has fully realized and unfolded the divinity whose germ is within him, finds the whole of this glory within his reach; but since none of us has yet done that, since we are only gradually rising towards that splendid consummation, it follows that none of us as yet can grasp that entirety.

But each draws from it and cognizes so much of it as he has by previous effort prepared himself to take. Different individuals bring very different capacities; they tell us in the East that each man brings his own cup, and some of the cups are large and some are small, but small or large every cup is filled to its utmost capacity; the sea of bliss holds far more than enough for all.

A man can look out upon all this glory and beauty only through the windows which he himself has made. Every one of these thought-forms is such a window, through which response may come to him from the forces without. If during his earth-life he has chiefly regarded physical things, then he has made for himself but few windows through which this higher glory can shine in upon him. Yet every man who is above the lowest savage must have had some touch of pure unselfish feeling, even if it were but once in all his life, and that will be a window for him now.

The ordinary man is not capable of any great activity in this mental world; his condition is chiefly receptive, and his vision of anything outside his own shell of thought is of the most limited character. He is surrounded by living forces, mighty angelic inhabitants of this glorious world, and many of their orders are very sensitive to certain aspirations of man and readily respond to them. But a man can take advantage of these only in so far as he has already prepared himself to profit by them, for his thoughts and aspirations are only along certain lines, and he cannot suddenly form new lines. There are many directions which the higher thought may take – some of them personal and some impersonal. Among the latter are art, music and philosophy; and a man whose interest lay along any one of these lines finds both measureless enjoyment and unlimited instruction waiting for him – that is, the amount of enjoyment and instruction is limited only by his power of perception.

We find a large number of people whose only higher thoughts are those connected with affection and devotion. If a man loves another deeply or if he feels strong devotion to a personal deity, he makes a strong mental image of that friend or of the deity, and the object of his feeling is often present in his mind. Inevitably he takes that mental image into the heaven-world with him, because it is to that level of matter that it naturally belongs.

Take first the case of affection. The love which forms and retains such an image is a very powerful force – a force which is strong enough to reach and to act upon the ego of his friend in the higher part of the mental world. It is that ego that is the real man whom he loves – not the physical body which is so partial a representation of him. The ego of the friend, feeling this vibration, at once and eagerly responds to it, and pours himself into the thought-form, which has been made for him; so that the man's friend is truly present with him more vividly than ever before. To this result it makes no difference whatever whether the friend is what we call living or dead; the appeal is made not to the fragment of the friend which is sometimes imprisoned in a physical body, but to the man himself on his own true level; and he always responds. A man who has a hundred friends can simultaneously and fully respond to the affection of every one of them, for no number of representations on a lower level can exhaust the infinity of the ego.

Thus every man in his heaven-life has around him all the friends for whose company he wishes, and they are for him always at their best, because he himself makes for them the thought-form through which they manifest to him. In our limited physical world we are so accustomed to thinking of our friend as only the limited manifestation which we know in the physical world, that it is at first difficult for us to realize the grandeur of the conception; when we can realize it, we shall see how much nearer we are in truth to our friends in the heaven-life than we ever were on earth. The same is true in the case of devotion. The man in the heaven-world is two great stages nearer to the object of his devotion than he was during physical life, and so his experiences are of a far more transcendent character.

In this mental world, as in the astral, there are seven subdivisions. The first, second and third are the habitat of the ego in his causal body, so the mental body contains matter of the remaining four only, and it is in those sections that his heaven-life is passed. Man does not, however, pass from one to the other of these, as is the case in the astral world, for there is nothing in this life corresponding to the rearrangement. Rather is the man drawn to the level which best corresponds to the degree of his development, and on that level he spends the whole of his life in the mental body. Each man makes his own conditions, so that the number of varieties is infinite.

Speaking broadly, we may say that the dominant characteristic observed in the lowest portion is unselfish family affection. Unselfish it must be, or it would find no place here; all selfish tinges, if there were any, worked out their results in the astral world. The dominant characteristic of the sixth level may be said to be anthropomorphical religious devotion; while that of the fifth section is devotion expressing itself in active work of some sort. All these – the fifth, sixth and seventh sub-divisions – are concerned with the working out of devotion to personalities (either to one's family and friends or to a personal deity) rather than the wider devotion to humanity for its own sake, which finds its expression in the next section. The activities of this fourth stage are varied. They can best be arranged in four main divisions: unselfish pursuit of spiritual knowledge; high philosophy or scientific thought; literary or artistic ability exercised for unselfish purposes; and service for the sake of service.

Even to this glorious heaven-life there comes an end, and then the mental body in its turn drops away as the others have done, and the man's life in his causal body begins. Here the man needs no windows, for this is his true home and all his walls have fallen away. The majority of men have as yet but very little consciousness at such a height as this; they rest dreamily unobservant and scarcely awake, but such vision as they have is true, however limited it may be by their lack of development. Still, every time they return, these limitations will be smaller, and they themselves will be greater; so that this truest life will be wider and fuller for them.

As this improvement continues, this causal life grows longer and longer, assuming an ever larger proportion as compared to the existence at lower levels. And as he grows, the man becomes capable not only of receiving but also of giving. Then indeed is his triumph approaching, for he is learning the lesson of the Christ, learning the crowning glory of sacrifice, the supreme delight of pouring out all his life for the helping of his fellowmen, the devotion of the self to the all, of celestial strength to human service, of all those splendid heavenly forces to the aid of the struggling sons of earth. That is part of the life that lies before us; these are some of the steps which even we who are still so near the bottom of the golden ladder may see rising above us, so that we may report them to those who have not seen as yet, in order that they too may open their eyes to the unimaginable splendour which surrounds them here and now in this dull daily life. This is part of the gospel of Theosophy – the certainty of this sublime future for all. It is certain because it is here already, because to inherit it we have only to fit ourselves for it.

Chapter VII
REINCARNATION

This life of the ego in his own world, which is so glorious and so fully satisfying for the developed man, plays but a very small part in the life of the ordinary person, for in his case the ego has not yet reached a sufficient stage of development to be awake in his causal body. In obedience to the law of Nature he has withdrawn into it, but in doing so he has lost the sensation of vivid life, and his restless desire to feel this once more pushes him in the direction of another descent into matter.

This is the scheme of evolution appointed for man at the present stage – that he shall develop by descending into grosser matter, and then ascend to carry back into himself the result of the experiences so obtained. His real life, therefore, covers millions of years, and what we are in the habit of calling a life is only one day of this greater existence. Indeed, it is in reality only a small part of one day; for a life of seventy years in the physical world is often succeeded by a period of twenty times that length spent in higher spheres.

Every one of us has a long line of these physical lives behind him, and the ordinary man has a fairly long line still in front of him. Each of such lives is a day at school. The ego puts upon himself his garment of flesh and goes forth into the school of the physical world to learn certain lessons. He learns them, or does not learn them, or partially learns them, as the case may be, during his schoolday of earth-life; then he lays aside the vesture of the flesh and returns home to his own level for rest and refreshment. In the morning of each new life he takes up again his lesson at the point where he left it the night before. Some lessons he may be able to learn in one day, while others may take him many days.

If he is an apt pupil and learns quickly what is needed, if he obtains an intelligent grasp of the rules of the school, and takes the trouble to adapt his conduct to them, his school-life is comparatively short, and when it is over he goes forth fully equipped into the real life of the higher worlds for which all this is only a preparation. Other egos are duller boys who do not learn so quickly; some of them do not understand the rules of the school, and through that ignorance are constantly breaking them; others are wayward, and even when they see the rules they cannot at once bring themselves to act in harmony with them. All of these have a longer school-life, and by their own actions they delay their entry upon the real life of the higher worlds.

For this is a school in which no pupil ever fails; every one must go on to the end. He has no choice as to that; but the length of time which he will take in qualifying himself for the higher examinations is left entirely to his own discretion. The wise pupil, seeing that school-life is not a thing in itself, but only a preparation for a more glorious and far wider life, endeavours to comprehend as fully as possible the rules of his school, and shapes his life in accordance with them as closely as he can, so that no time may be lost in the learning of whatever lessons are necessary. He co-operates intelligently with the Teachers, and sets himself to do the maximum of work which is possible for him, in order that as soon as he can he may come of age and enter into his kingdom as a glorified ego.

Theosophy explains to us the laws under which this school-life must be lived, and in that way gives a great advantage to its students. The first great law is that of evolution. Every man has to become a perfect man, to unfold to the fullest degree the divine possibilities which lie latent within him, for that unfoldment is the object of the entire scheme so far as he is concerned. This law of evolution steadily presses him onward to higher and higher achievements. The wise man tries to anticipate its demands – to run ahead of the necessary curriculum, for in that way he not only avoids all collision with it, but he obtains the maximum of assistance from its action. The man who lags behind in the race of life finds its steady pressure constantly constraining him – a pressure which, if resisted, rapidly becomes painful. Thus the laggard on the path of evolution has always the sense of being hunted and driven by his fate, while the man who intelligently co-operates is left perfectly free to choose the direction in which he shall move, so long as it is onward and upward.

The second great law under which this evolution is taking place is the law of cause and effect. There can be no effect without its cause, and every cause must produce its effect. They are in fact not two but one, for the effect is really part of the cause, and he who sets one in motion sets the other also. There is in Nature no such idea as that of reward or punishment, but only of cause and effect. Anyone can see this in connection with mechanics or chemistry; the clairvoyant sees it equally clearly with regard to the problems of evolution. The same law obtains in the higher as in the lower worlds; there, as here, the angle of reflection is always equal to the angle of incidence. It is a law of mechanics that action and reaction are equal and opposite. In the almost infinitely finer matter of the higher worlds the reaction is by no means always instantaneous; it may sometimes be spread over long periods of time, but it returns inevitably and exactly.

Just as certain in its working as the mechanical law in the physical world is the higher law, according to which the man who sends out a good thought or does a good action receives good in return, while the man who sends out an evil thought or does an evil action, receives evil in return with equal accuracy – once more, not in the least a reward or punishment administered by some external will, but simply as the definite and mechanical result of his own activity. Man has learnt to appreciate a mechanical result in the physical world, because the reaction is usually almost immediate and can be seen by him. He does not invariably understand the reaction in the higher worlds because that takes a wider sweep, and often returns not in this physical life, but in some future one.

The action of this law affords the explanation of a number of the problems of ordinary life. It accounts for the different destinies imposed upon people, and also for the differences in the people themselves. If one man is clever in a certain direction and another is stupid, it is because in a previous life the clever man has devoted much effort to practise in that particular direction, while the stupid man is trying it for the first time. The genius and the precocious child are examples not of the favouritism of some deity but of the result produced by previous lives of application. All the varied circumstances which surrounded us are the result of our own actions in the past, precisely as are the qualities of which we find ourselves in possession. We are what we have made ourselves, and our circumstances are such as we have deserved.

There is, however, a certain adjustment or apportionment of these effects. Though the law is a natural law and mechanical in its operation, there are nevertheless certain great Angels who are concerned with its administration. They cannot change by one feather-weight the amount of the result which follows upon any given thought or act, but they can within certain limits expedite or delay its action, and decide what form it shall take.

If this were not done there would be at least a possibility that in his earlier stages the man might blunder so seriously that the results of his blundering might be more than he could bear. The plan of the Deity is to give man a limited amount of free-will; if he uses that small amount well, he earns the right to a little more next time; if he uses it badly, suffering comes upon him as the result of such evil use, and he finds himself restrained by the result of his previous actions. As the man learns how to use his free-will, more and more of it is entrusted to him, so that he can acquire for himself practically unbounded freedom in the direction of good, but his power to do wrong is strictly restricted. He can progress as rapidly as he will, but he cannot wreck his life in his ignorance. In the earlier stages of the savage life of primitive man it is natural that there should be on the whole more of evil than of good, and if the entire result of his actions came at once upon a man as yet so little developed, it might well crush the newly evolved powers which are still so feeble.

Besides this, the effects of his actions are varied in character. While some of them produce immediate results, others need much more time for their action, and so it comes to pass that as the man develops he has above him a hovering cloud of undischarged results, some of them good, some of them bad. Out of this mass (which we may regard for purposes of analogy much as though it were a debt owing to the powers of Nature) a certain amount falls due in each of his successive births; and that amount, so assigned, may be thought of as the man's destiny for that particular life.

All that it means is that a certain amount of joy and a certain amount of suffering are due to him, and will unavoidably happen to him; how he will meet this destiny and what use he will make of it, that is left entirely to his own option. It is a certain amount of force which has to work itself out. Nothing can prevent the action of that force, but its action may always be modified by the application of a new force in another direction, just as is the case in mechanics. The result of past evil is like any other debt; it may be paid in one large cheque upon the bank of life – by some one supreme catastrophe; or it may be paid in a number of smaller notes, in minor troubles and worries; in some cases it may even be paid in the small change of a great number of petty annoyances. But one thing is quite certain – that, in some form or other, paid it will have to be.

The conditions of our present life, then, are absolutely the result of our own action in the past; and the other side of that statement is that our actions in this life are building up conditions for the next one. A man who finds himself limited either in powers or in outer circumstances may not always be able to make himself or his conditions all that he would wish in this life; but he can certainly secure for the next one whatever he chooses.

Man's every action ends not with himself, but invariably affects others around him. In some cases this effect may be comparatively trivial, while in others it may be of the most serious character. The trivial results, whether good or bad, are simply small debits or credits in our account with Nature; but the greater effects, whether good or bad, make a personal account which is to be settled with the individual concerned.

A man who gives a meal to a hungry beggar, or cheers him by a kindly word, will receive the result of his good action as part of a kind of general fund of Nature's benefits; but one who by some good action changes the whole current of another man's life will assuredly have to meet that same man again in a future life, in order that he who has been benefited may have the opportunity of repaying the kindness that has been done to him. One who causes annoyance to another will suffer proportionately for it somewhere, somehow, in the future, though he may never meet again the man whom he has troubled; but one who does serious harm to another, one who wrecks his life or retards his evolution, must certainly meet his victim again at some later point in the course of their lives, so that he may have the opportunity, by kindly and self-sacrificing service, of counterbalancing the wrong which he has done. In short, large debts must be paid personally, but small ones go into the general fund.

These then are the principal factors which determine the next birth of the man. First acts the great law of evolution, and its tendency is to press the man into that position in which he can most easily develop the qualities which he most needs. For the purposes of the general scheme, humanity is divided into great races, called root-races, which rule and occupy the world successively. The great Aryan or Indo-Caucasian race, which at the present moment includes the most advanced of Earth's inhabitants, is one of these. That which came before it in the order of evolution was the Mongolian race, usually called in Theosophical books Atlantean because the continent from which it ruled the world lay where now roll the waters of the Atlantic ocean. Before that came the Negroid race, some of whose descendants still exist, though by this time much mingled with offshoots of later races. From each of these great root-races there are many offshoots which we call sub-races – such, for example, as the Roman races or the Teutonic; and each of the sub-races in turn divides itself into branch-races, such as the French and the Italians, the English and the Germans.

These arrangements are made in order that for each ego there may be a wide choice of varying conditions and surroundings. Each race is especially adapted to develop within its people one or other of the qualities which are needed in the course of evolution. In every nation there exist an almost infinite number of diverse conditions, riches and poverty, a wide field of opportunities or a total lack of them, facilities for development or conditions under which development is difficult or well-nigh impossible. Amidst all these infinite possibilities the pressure of the law of evolution tends to guide the man to precisely those which best suit his needs at the stage at which he happens to be.

But the action of this law is limited by that other law of which we spoke, the law of cause and effect. The man's actions in the past may not have been such as to deserve (if we may put it so) the best possible opportunities; he may have set in motion in his past certain forces the inevitable result of which will be to produce limitations; and these limitations may operate to prevent his receiving that best possible of opportunities, and so as the result of his own actions in the past he may have to put up with the second best. So we may say that the action of the law of evolution, which if left to itself would do the very best possible for every man, is restrained by the man's own previous actions.

An important feature in that limitation – one which may act most powerfully for good or for evil – is the influence of the group of egos with which the man has made definite links in the past – those with whom he has formed strong ties of love or hate, of helping or of injury – those souls whom he must meet again because of connections made with them in days of long ago. His relation with them is a factor which must be taken into consideration before it can be determined where and how he shall be reborn.

The Will of the Deity is man's evolution. The effort of that nature which is an expression of the Deity is to give the man whatever is most suitable for that evolution; but this is conditioned by the man's deserts in the past and by the links which he has already formed. It may be assumed that a man descending into incarnation could learn the lessons necessary for that life in any one of a hundred positions. From half of these or more than half he may be debarred by the consequences of some of his many and varied actions in the past. Among the few possibilities which remain open to him, the choice of one possibility in particular may be determined by the presence in that family or in that neighbourhood of other egos upon whom he has a claim for services rendered, or to whom he in his turn owes a debt of love.

Chapter VIII
THE PURPOSE OF LIFE

To fulfil our duty in the divine scheme we must try to understand not only that scheme as a whole, but the special part that man is intended to play in it. The divine outbreathing reached its deepest immersion in matter in the mineral kingdom, but it reaches its ultimate point of differentiation not at the lowest level of materiality, but at the entrance into the human kingdom on the upward arc of evolution. We have thus to realize three stages in the course of this evolution.

(a) The downward arc in which the tendency is towards differentiation and also towards greater materiality. In this stage spirit is involving itself in matter, in order that it may learn to receive impressions through it.

(b) The earlier part of the upward arc, in which the tendency is still towards greater differentiation, but at the same time towards spiritualization and escape from materiality. In this stage the spirit is learning to dominate matter and to see it as an expression of itself.

(c) The later part of the upward arc, when differentiation has been finally accomplished, and the tendency is towards unity as well as towards greater spirituality. In this stage the spirit, having learnt perfectly how to receive impression through matter and how to express itself through it, and having awakened its dormant powers, learns to use these powers rightly in the service of the Deity.

The object of the whole previous evolution has been to produce the ego as a manifestation of the Monad. Then the ego in its turn evolves by putting itself down into a succession of personalities. Men who do not understand this look upon the personality as the self, and consequently live for it alone, and try to regulate their lives for what appears to be its temporary advantage. The man who understands realizes that the only important thing is the life of the ego, and that its progress is the object for which the temporary personality must be used. Therefore when he has to decide between two possible courses he thinks not, as the ordinary man might: "Which will bring the greater pleasure and profit to me as a personality?" but "Which will bring greater progress to me as an ego?" Experience soon teaches him that nothing can ever be really good for him, or for anyone, which is not good for all, and so presently he learns to forget himself altogether, and to ask only what will be best for humanity as a whole.

Clearly then at this stage of evolution whatever tends to unity, whatever tends to spirituality, is in accord with the plan of the Deity for us, and is therefore right for us, while whatever tends to separateness or to materiality is equally certainly wrong for us. There are thoughts and emotions which tend to unity, such as love, sympathy, reverence, benevolence; there are others which tend to disunion, such as hatred, jealousy, envy, pride, cruelty, fear. Obviously the former group are for us the right, the latter group are for us the wrong. In all these thoughts and feelings which are clearly wrong, we recognize one dominant note, the thought of self; while in all those which are clearly right we recognize that the thought is turned toward others, and that the personal self is forgotten. Wherefore we see that selfishness is the one great wrong, and that perfect unselfishness is the crown of all virtue. This gives us at once a rule of life. The man who wishes intelligently to co-operate with the Divine Will must lay aside all thought of the advantage or pleasure of the personal self, and must devote himself exclusively to carrying out that Will by working for the welfare and happiness of others.

This is a high ideal, and difficult of attainment, because there lies behind us such a long history of selfishness. Most of us are as yet far from the purely altruistic attitude; how are we to go to work to attain it, lacking as we do the necessary intensity in so many of the good qualities, and possessing so many which are undesirable?

Here comes into operation the great law of cause and effect to which I have already referred. Just as we can confidently appeal to the laws of Nature in the physical world, so may we also appeal to these laws of the higher world. If we find evil qualities within us, they have grown up by slow degrees through ignorance and through self-indulgence. Now that the ignorance is dispelled by knowledge, now that in consequence we recognize the quality as an evil, the method of getting rid of it lies obviously before us.

For each of these vices there is a contrary virtue; if we find one of them rearing its head within us, let us immediately determine deliberately to develop within ourselves the contrary virtue. If a man realizes that in the past he has been selfish, that means that he has set up within himself the habit of thinking of himself first and pleasing himself, of consulting his own convenience or his pleasure without due thought of the effect upon others; let him set to work purposefully to form the exactly opposite habit, to make a practice before doing anything of thinking how it will affect all those around him; let him set himself habitually to please others, even though it be at the cost of trouble or privation for himself. This also in time will become a habit, and by developing it he will have killed out the other.

If a man finds himself full of suspicion, ready always to assign evil motives to the actions of those about him, let him set himself steadily to cultivate trust in his fellows, to give them credit always for the highest possible motives. It may be said that a man who does this will lay himself open to be deceived, and that in many cases his confidence will be misplaced. That is a small matter; it is far better for him that he should sometimes be deceived as a result of his trust in his fellows than that he should save himself from such deception by maintaining a constant attitude of suspicion. Besides, confidence begets faithfulness. A man who is trusted will generally prove himself worthy of the trust, whereas a man who is suspected is likely presently to justify the suspicion.

If a man finds in himself the tendency towards avarice, let him go out of his way to be especially generous; if he finds himself irritable, let him definitely train himself in calmness; if he finds himself devoured by curiosity, let him deliberately refuse again and again to gratify that curiosity; if he is liable to fits of depression, let him persistently cultivate cheerfulness, even under the most adverse circumstances.

In every case the existence of an evil quality in the personality means a lack of the corresponding good quality in the ego. The shortest way to get rid of that evil and to prevent its reappearance is to fill the gap in the ego, and the good quality which is thus developed will show itself as an integral part of the man's character through all his future lives. An ego cannot be evil, but he can be imperfect. The qualities which he develops cannot be other than good qualities, and when they are well defined they show themselves in each of all his numerous personalities, and consequently those personalities can never be guilty of the vices opposite to these qualities; but where there is a gap in the ego, where there is a quality undeveloped, there is nothing inherent in the personality to check the growth of the opposite vice; and since others in the world about him already possess that vice, and man is an imitative animal, it is quite probable that it will speedily manifest itself in him. This vice, however, belongs to the vehicles only and not to the man inside. In these vehicles its repetition may set up a momentum which is hard to conquer; but if the ego bestirs himself to create in himself the opposite virtue, the vice is cut off at its root, and can no longer exist – neither in this life nor in all the lives that are to come.

A man who is trying to evolve these qualities in himself will find certain obstacles in his way – obstacles which he must learn to surmount. One of these is the critical spirit of the age – the disposition to find fault with a thing, to belittle everything, to look for faults in everything and everyone. The exact opposite of this is what is needed for progress. He who wishes to move rapidly along the path of evolution must learn to see good in everything – to see the latent Deity in everything and in everyone. Only so can he help those other people – only so can he get the best out of those other things.

Another obstacle is the lack of perseverance. We tend in these days to be impatient; if we try any plan we expect immediate results from it, and if we do not get them, we give up that plan and try something else. That is not the way to make progress in occultism. The effort which we are making is to compress into one or two lives the evolution which would naturally take perhaps a hundred lives. That is not the sort of undertaking in which immediate results are to be expected. We attempt to uproot an evil habit, and we find it hard work; why? Because we have indulged in that practice for, perhaps, twenty thousand years; one cannot shake off the custom of twenty thousand years in a day or two. We have allowed that habit to gain an enormous momentum, and before we can set up a force in the opposite direction we have to overcome that momentum. That cannot be done in a moment, but it is absolutely certain that it *will* be done eventually, if we persevere, because the momentum, however strong it may be, is a finite quantity, whereas the power that we can bring to bear against it is the infinite power of the human will, which can make renewed efforts day after day, year after year, even life after life if necessary.

Another great difficulty in our way is the lack of clearness in our thought. People in the West are little used to clear thought with regard to religious matters. Everything is vague and nebulous. For occult development vagueness and nebulosity will not do. Our conceptions must be clear-cut and our thought-images definite. Other necessary characteristics are calmness and cheerfulness; these are rare in modern life, but are absolute essentials for the work which we are here undertaking.

The process of building a character is as scientific as that of developing one's muscles. Many a man, finding himself with certain muscles flabby and powerless takes that as his natural condition, and regards their weakness as a kind of destiny imposed upon him; but anyone who understands a little of the human body is aware that by continued exercise those muscles can be brought into a state of health and the whole body eventually put in order. In exactly the same way, many a man finds himself possessed of a bad temper or a tendency to avarice or suspicion or self-indulgence, and when in consequence of any of these vices he commits some great mistake or does some great harm he offers it as an excuse that he is a hasty-tempered man, or that he possesses this or that quality by nature – implying that therefore he cannot help it.

In this case just as in the other the remedy is in his own hands. Regular exercise of the right kind will develop a certain muscle, and regular mental exercise of the right kind will develop a missing quality in a man's character. The ordinary man does not realize that he can do this, and even if he sees that he can do it, he does not see why he should, for it means much effort and much self-repression. He knows of no adequate motive for undertaking a task so laborious and painful.

The motive is supplied by the knowledge of the truth. One who gains an intelligent comprehension of the direction of evolution feels it not only his interest but his privilege and his delight to co-operate with it. One who wills the end wills also the means; in order to be able to do good work for the world he must develop within himself the necessary strength and the necessary qualities. Therefore he who wishes to reform the world must first of all reform himself. He must learn to give up altogether the attitude of insisting upon rights, and must devote himself utterly to the most earnest performance of his duties. He must learn to regard every connection with his fellow-man as an opportunity to help that fellow-man, or in some way to do him good.

One who studies these subjects intelligently cannot but realize the tremendous power of thought, and the necessity for its efficient control. All action springs from thought, for even when it is done (as we say) without thought, it is the instinctive expression of the thoughts, desires and feelings which the man has allowed to grow luxuriantly within himself in earlier days.

The wise man, therefore, will watch his thought with the greatest of care, for in it he possesses a powerful instrument, for the right use of which he is responsible. It is his duty to govern his thought, lest it should be allowed to run riot and to do evil to himself, and to others; it is his duty also to develop his thought-power, because by means of it a vast amount of actual and active good can be done. Thus controlling his thought and his action, thus eliminating from himself all evil and unfolding in himself all good qualities, the man presently raises himself far above the level of his fellows, and stands out conspicuously among them as one who is working on the side of good as against evil, of evolution as against stagnation.

The Members of the great Hierarchy, in whose hands is the evolution of the world, are watching always for such men in order that They may train them to help in the great work. Such a man inevitably attracts Their attention, and They begin to use him as an instrument in Their work. If he proves himself a good and efficient instrument, presently They will offer him definite training as an apprentice, that by helping Them in the world-business which They have to do he may some day become even as They are, and join the mighty Brotherhood to which They belong.

But for an honour so great as this mere ordinary goodness will not suffice. True, a man must be good first of all, or it would be hopeless to think of using him, but in addition to being good he must be wise and strong. What is needed is not merely a good man, but a great spiritual power. Not only must the candidate have cast aside all ordinary weaknesses but he must have acquired strong positive qualities before he can offer himself to Them with any hope that he will be accepted. He must live no longer as a blundering and selfish personality, but as an intelligent ego who comprehends the part which he has to play in the great scheme of the universe. He must have forgotten himself utterly; he must have resigned all thought of worldly profit or pleasure or advancement; he must be willing to sacrifice everything, and himself first of all, for the sake of the work that has to be done. He may be *in* the world, but he must not be *of* the world. He must be careless utterly of its opinion. For the sake of helping man he must make himself something more than man. Radiant, rejoicing, strong, he must live but for the sake of others and to be an expression of the love of God in the world. A high ideal, yet not too high; possible, because there are men who have achieved it.

When a man has succeeded in unfolding his latent possibilities so far that he attracts the attention of the Masters of the Wisdom, one of Them will probably receive him as an apprentice upon probation. The period of probation is usually seven years, but may be either shortened or lengthened at the discretion of the Master. At the end of that time, if his work has been satisfactory, he becomes what it commonly called the accepted pupil. This brings him into close relations with his Master, so that the vibrations of the latter constantly play upon him, and he gradually learns to look at everything as the Master looks at it. After yet another interval, if he proves himself entirely worthy, he may be drawn into a still closer relationship, when he is called the son of the Master.

These three stages mark his relationship to his own Master only, not to the Brotherhood as a whole. The Brotherhood admits a man to its ranks only when he has fitted himself to pass the first of the great Initiations.

This entry into the Brotherhood of Those who rule the world may be thought of as the third of the great critical points in man's evolution. The first of these is when he becomes man – when he individualizes out of the animal kingdom and obtains a causal body. The second is what is called by the Christian "conversion", by the Hindu "the acquirement of discrimination", and by the Buddhist "the opening of the doors of the mind". That is the point at which he realizes the great facts of life, and turns away from the pursuit of selfish ends in order to move intentionally along with the great current of evolution in obedience to the divine Will. The third point is the most important of all, for the Initiation which admits him to the ranks of the Brotherhood also insures him against the possibility of failure to fulfil the divine purpose in the time appointed for it. Hence those who have reached this point are called in the Christian system the "elect", the "saved" or the "safe", and in the Buddhist scheme " those who have entered on the stream". For those who have reached this point have made themselves absolutely certain of reaching a further point also – that of Adeptship, at which they pass into a type of evolution which is definitely Superhuman.

The man who has become an Adept has fulfilled the divine Will so far as this chain of worlds is concerned. He has reached, even already at the midmost point of the aeon of evolution, the stage prescribed for man's attainment at the end of it. Therefore he is at liberty to spend the remainder of that time either in helping his fellowmen or in even more splendid work in connection with other and higher evolutions. He who has not yet been initiated is still in danger of being left behind by our present wave of evolution, and dropping into the next one – the "æonian condemnation" of which the Christ spoke, which has been mistranslated "eternal damnation". It is from this fate of possible aeonian failure – that is, failure for this age, or dispensation, or life-wave – that the man who attains Initiation is "safe". He has "entered upon the stream" which now *must* bear him on to Adeptship in this present age, though it is still possible for him by his actions to hasten or delay his progress along the Path which he is treading.

That first Initiation corresponds to the matriculation which admits a man to a University, and the attainment of Adeptship to the taking of a degree at the end of a course. Continuing the simile, there are three intermediate examinations, which are usually spoken of as the second, third, and fourth Initiations, Adeptship being the fifth. A general idea of the line of this higher evolution may be obtained by studying the list of what are called in Buddhist books "the fetters" which must be cast off – the qualities of which a man must rid himself as he treads this Path. These are: the delusion of separateness; doubt or uncertainty; superstition; attachment to enjoyment; the possibility of hatred; desire for life, either in this or the higher worlds; pride; agitation or irritability; and ignorance. The man who reaches the Adept level has exhausted all the possibilities of moral development, and so the future evolution which still lies before him can only mean still wider knowledge and still more wonderful spiritual powers.

Chapter IX
THE PLANETARY CHAINS

The scheme of evolution of which our Earth forms a part is not the only one in our solar system, for ten separate chains of globes exist in that system which are all of them theatres of somewhat similar progress. Each of these schemes of evolution is taking place upon a chain of globes, and in the course of each scheme its chain of globes goes through seven incarnations. The plan, alike of each scheme as a whole and of the successive incarnations of its chain of globes, is to dip step by step more deeply into matter, and then to rise step by step out of it again.

Each chain consists of seven globes, and both globes and chains observe the rule of descending into matter and then rising out of it again. In order to make this comprehensible let us take as an example the chain to which our Earth belongs. At the present time it is in its fourth or most material incarnation, and therefore three of its globes belong to the physical world, two to the astral world, and two to the lower part of the mental world. The wave of divine Life passes in succession from globe to globe of this chain, beginning with one of the highest, descending gradually to the lowest and then climbing again to the same level as that at which it began.

Let us for convenience of reference label the seven globes by the earlier letters of the alphabet, and number the incarnations in order. Thus, as this is the fourth incarnation of our chain, the first globe in this incarnation will be 4A, the second 4B, the third 4C, the fourth (which is our Earth) 4D, and so on.

These globes are not all composed of physical matter. 4A contains no matter lower than that of the mental world; it has its counterpart in all the worlds higher than that, but nothing below it. 4B exists in the astral world; but 4C is a physical globe, visible to our telescopes, and is in fact the planet which we know as Mars. Globe 4D is our own Earth, on which the life-wave of the chain is at present in action. Globe 4E is the planet which we call Mercury – also in the physical world. Globe 4F is in the astral world, corresponding on the ascending arc to globe 4B in the descent; while globe 4G corresponds to globe 4A in having its lowest manifestation in the lower part of the mental world. Thus it will be seen that we have a scheme of globes starting in the lower mental world, dipping through the astral into the physical and then rising into the lower mental through the astral again.

Just as the succession of the globes in a chain constitutes a descent into matter and an ascent from it again, so do the successive incarnations of a chain. We have described the condition of affairs in the fourth incarnation; looking back at the third, we find that that commences not on the lower level of the mental world but on the higher. Globes 3A and 3G, then, are both of higher mental matter, while globes 3B and 3F are at the lower mental level. Globes 3C and 3E belong to the astral world, and only globe 3D is visible in the physical world. Although this third incarnation of our chain is long past, the corpse of this physical globe 3D is still visible to us in the shape of that dead planet the Moon, whence that third incarnation is usually called the lunar chain.

The fifth incarnation of our chain, which still lies very far in the future, will correspond to the third. In that, globes 5A and 5G will be built of higher mental matter, globes 5B and 5F of lower mental, globes 5C and 5E of astral matter, and only globe 5D will be in the physical world. This planet 5D is of course not yet in existence.

The other incarnations of the chain follow the same general rule of gradually decreasing materiality; 2A, 2G, 6A and 6G are all in the intuitional world; 2B, 2F, 6B and 6F are all in the higher part of the mental world; 2C, 2E, 6C and 6E are in the lower part of the mental world; 2D and 6D are in the astral world. In the same way 1A, 1G, 7A and 7G belong to the spiritual world; 1B, 1F, 7B and 7F are in the intuitional world; 1C, 1E, 7C and 7E are in the higher part of the mental world; 1D and 7D are in the lower part of the mental world.

Thus it will be seen that not only does the life-wave in passing through one chain of globes dip down into matter and rise out of it again, but the chain itself in its successive incarnations does exactly the same thing.

There are ten schemes of evolution at present existing in our solar system, but only seven of them are at the stage where they have planets in the physical world. These are: (1) that of an unrecognized planet Vulcan, very near the sun, about which we have very little definite information. It was seen by the astronomer Herschel, but is now said to have disappeared. We at first understood that it was in its third incarnation; but it is now regarded as possible that it has recently passed from its fifth to its sixth chain, which would account for its alleged disappearance; (2) that of Venus, which is in its fifth incarnation, and also therefore, has only one visible globe; (3) that of the Earth, Mars and Mercury, which has three visible planets because it is in its fourth incarnation; (4) that of Jupiter, (5) that of Saturn, (6) that of Uranus, all in their third incarnations ; and (7) that of Neptune and the two unnamed planets beyond its orbit, which is in its fourth incarnation, and therefore has three physical planets as we have.

In each incarnation of a chain (commonly called a chain-period) the wave of divine Life moves seven times round the chain of seven planets, and each such movement is spoken of as a round. The time that the life-wave stays upon each planet is known as a world-period, and in the course of a world-period there are seven great root-races. As has been previously explained, these are subdivided into sub-races, and those again into branch-races. For convenience of reference we may state this in tabular form:

7 Branch-Races	make 1 Sub-Race
7 Sub-Races	make 1 Root-Race
7 Root-Races	make 1 World-Period
7 World-Periods	make 1 Round
7 Rounds	make 1 Chain-Period
7 Chain-Periods	make 1 Scheme of Evolution
10 Schemes of Evolution	make 1 Our Solar System

It is clear that the fourth root-race of the fourth globe of the fourth round of a fourth chain-period would be the central point of a whole scheme of evolution, and we find ourselves at the present moment only a little past that point. The Aryan race, to which we belong, is the fifth root-race of the fourth globe, so that the actual middle point fell in the time of the last great root-race, the Atlantean. Consequently the human race as a whole is very little more than half-way through its evolution, and those few souls who are already nearing Adeptship, which is the end and crown of this evolution, are very far in advance of their fellows.

How do they come to be so far in advance? Partly and in some cases because they have worked harder, but usually because they are older egos – because they were individualized out of the animal kingdom at an earlier date, and so have had more time for the human part of their evolution.

Any given wave of life sent forth from the Deity usually spends a chain-period in each of the great kingdoms of Nature. That which in our first chain was ensouling the first elemental kingdom must have ensouled the second of those kingdoms in the second chain, in the third of them in the Moon-chain, and is now in the mineral kingdom in the fourth chain. In the future fifth chain it will ensoul the vegetable kingdom, in the sixth the animal, and in the seventh it will attain humanity.

From this it follows that we ourselves represented the mineral kingdom on the first chain, the vegetable on the second, and the animal on the lunar chain. There some of us attained our individualization, and so we were enabled to enter this Earth-chain as men. Others who were a little more backward did not succeed in attaining it, and so had to be born into this chain as animals for a while before they could reach humanity. Not all of mankind, however, entered this chain together. When the lunar chain came to its end the humanity upon it stood at various levels. Not Adeptship, but what is now for us the fourth step on the Path, was the goal appointed for that chain. Those who had attained it (commonly called in Theosophical literature the Lords of the Moon) had, as is usual, seven choices before them as to the way in which they would serve. Only one of those choices brought them, or rather a few of them, over into this Earth-chain to act as guides and teachers to the earlier races. A considerable proportion – a vast proportion, indeed – of the Moon-men had not attained that level, and consequently had to reappear in this Earth-chain as humanity. Besides this, a great mass of the animal kingdom of the Moon-chain was surging up to the level of the individualization, and some of its members had already reached it, while many others had not. These latter needed further animal incarnations upon the Earth-chain, and for the moment may be put aside.

There were many classes even among the humanity, and the manner in which these distributed themselves over the Earth-chain needs some explanation. It is the general rule that those who have attained the highest possible in any chain on any globe, in any root-race, are not born into the beginning of the next chain, globe or race, respectively. The earlier stages are always for the backward entities, and only when they have already passed through a good deal of evolution and are beginning to approach the level of those others who had done better, do the latter descend into incarnation and join them once more. That is to say, almost the earlier half of any period of evolution, whether it be a race, a globe or a chain, seems to be devoted to bringing the backward people up to nearly the level of those who have got on better; then these latter also (who, in the meantime, have been resting in great enjoyment in the mental world) descend into incarnation along with the others, and they press on together until the end of the period.

Thus the first of the egos from the Moon who entered the Earth-chain were by no means the most advanced.

Indeed they may be described as the least advanced of those who had succeeded in attaining humanity – the animal-men. Coming as they did into a chain of new globes, freshly aggregated, they had to establish the forms in all the different kingdoms of Nature. This needs to be done at the beginning of the first round in a new chain, but never after that; for though the life-wave is centred only upon one of the seven globes of a chain at any given time, yet life has not entirely departed from the other globes. At the present moment, for example, the life-wave of our chain is centred on this Earth, but on the other two physical globes of our chain, Mars and Mercury, life still exists. There is still a population, human, animal and vegetable, and consequently when the life-wave goes round again to either of those planets there will be no necessity for the creation of new forms. The old types are already there, and all that will happen will be a sudden marvellous fecundity, so that the various kingdoms will quickly increase and multiply, and make a rapidly increasing population instead of a stationary one.

It was, then, the animal-men, the lowest class of human beings of the Moon-chain, who established the forms in the first round of the Earth-chain. Pressing closely after them were the highest of the lunar animal kingdom, who were soon ready to occupy the forms which had just been made. In the second journey round the seven globes of the Earth-chain, the animal-men who had been the most backward of the lunar humanity were leaders of this terrene humanity, the highest of the moon-animals making its less developed grades. The same thing went on in the third round of the Earth-chain, more and more of the lunar animals attaining individualization and joining the human rank, until in the middle of that round on this very globe D which we call the Earth, a higher class of human beings – the Second Order of Moon-men – descended into incarnation and at once took the lead.

When we come to the fourth, our present round, we find the First Order of the Moon-men pouring in upon us – all the highest and the best of the lunar humanity who had only just fallen short of success. Some of those who had already, even on the Moon, entered upon the Path soon attained its end, became Adepts and passed away from the Earth. Some few others who had not been quite so far advanced have attained Adeptship only comparatively recently – that is, within the last few thousand years, and these are the Adepts of the present day. We, who find ourselves in the higher races of humanity now, were several stages behind Them, but the opportunity lies before us of following in Their steps if we will.

The evolution of which we have been speaking is that of the Ego himself, of what might be called the soul of man; but at the same time there has been also an evolution to the body. The forms built in the first round were very different from any of which we know anything now. Properly speaking, those which were made on our physical earth can scarcely be called forms at all, for they were constructed of etheric matter only, and resembled vague, drifting and almost shapeless clouds. In the second round they were definitely physical, but still shapeless and light enough to float about in currents of wind.

Only in the third round did they begin to bear any kind of resemblance to man as we know him today. The very methods of reproduction of those primitive forms differed from those of humanity today, and far more resembled those which we now find only in very much lower types of life. Man in those early days was androgynous, and a definite separation into sexes took place only about the middle of the third round. From that time onward until now the shape of man has been steadily evolving along definitely human lines, becoming smaller and more compact than it was, learning to stand upright instead of stooping and crawling, and generally differentiating itself from the animal forms out of which it had been evolved.

One curious break in the regularity of this evolution deserves mention. On this globe, in this fourth round, there was a departure from the straightforward scheme of evolution. This being the middle globe of a middle round, the midmost point of evolution upon it marked the last moment at which it was possible for members of what had been the lunar animal kingdom to attain individualization. Consequently a sort of strong effort was made – a special scheme was arranged to give a final chance to as many as possible. The conditions of the first and second rounds were specially reproduced in place of the first and second races – conditions of which in the earlier rounds these backward egos had not been able fully to take advantage. Now, with the additional evolution, which they had undergone during the third round, some of them were able to take such advantage, and so they rushed in at the very last moment before the door was shut, and became just human. Naturally they will not reach any high level of human development, but at least when they try again in some future chain it will be some advantage to them to have had even this slight experience of human life.

Our terrestrial evolution received a most valuable stimulus from the assistance given to us by our sister globe, Venus. Venus is at present in the fifth incarnation of its chain, and in the seventh round of that incarnation, so that its inhabitants are a whole chain-period and a half in front of us in evolution. Since, therefore, its people are so much more developed than ours, it was thought desirable that certain Adepts from the Venus evolution should be transferred to our Earth in order to assist in the specially busy time just before the closing of the door, in the middle of the fourth root-race.

These august Beings have been called the Lords of the Flame and the Children of the Fire-mist, and They have produced a wonderful effect upon our evolution. The intellect of which we are so proud is almost entirely due to Their presence, for in the natural course of events, the next round, the fifth, should be that of intellectual advancement, and in this our present fourth round we should be devoting ourselves chiefly to the cultivation of the emotions. We are therefore in reality a long way in advance of the programme marked out for us; and such advance is entirely due to the assistance given by these great Lords of the Flame. Most of Them stayed with us only through that critical period of our history; a few still remain to hold the highest offices of the Great White Brotherhood until the time when men of our own evolution shall have risen to such a height as to be capable of relieving their august Visitors.

The evolution lying before us is both of the life and of the form; for in future rounds, while the egos will be steadily growing in power, wisdom and love, the physical forms also will be more beautiful and more perfect than they have ever yet been. We have in this world at the present time men at widely differing stages of evolution, and it is clear that there are vast hosts of savages who are far behind the great civilized races of the world – so far behind that it is quite impossible that they can overtake them. Later on in the course of our evolution a point will be reached at which it is no longer possible for those undeveloped souls to advance side by side with the others, so that it will be necessary that a division should be made.

The proceeding is exactly analogous to the sorting out by a schoolmaster of the boys in his class. During the school year he has to prepare his boys for a certain examination, and by perhaps the middle of that school year he knows quite well which of them will pass it. If he should have in his class some who are hopelessly behind the rest, he might reasonably say to them when the middle period was reached:

"It is quite useless for you to continue with your fellows, for the more difficult lessons which I shall now have to give will be entirely unintelligible to you. It is impossible that you can learn enough in the time to pass the examination, so that the effort would only be a useless strain for you, and meantime you would be a hindrance to the rest of the class. It is therefore far better for you to give up striving after the impossible, and to take up again the work of the lower class which you did not do perfectly, and then to offer yourselves for this examination along with next year's class, for what is now impossible for you will then be easy."

This is in effect exactly what is said at a certain stage in our future evolution, to the most backward egos. They drop out of this year's class and come along with the next one. This is the "æonian condemnation" to which reference was made a little while ago. It is computed that about two-fifths of humanity will drop out of the class in this way, leaving the remaining three-fifths to go on with far greater rapidity to the glorious destinies which lie before them.

Chapter X
THE RESULT OF THEOSOPHICAL STUDY

"Members of the Theosophical Society study these truths and Theosophists endeavour to live them." What manner of man then is the true Theosophist in consequence of his knowledge? What is the result in his daily life of all this study?

Finding that there is a Supreme Power who is directing the course of evolution, and that He is all-wise and all-loving, the Theosophist sees that everything which exists within this scheme must be intended to further its progress. He realizes that the scripture which tells us that all things are working together for good, is not indulging in a flight of poetic fancy or voicing a pious hope, but stating a scientific fact. The final attainment of unspeakable glory is an absolute certainty for every son of man, whatever may be his present condition; but that is by no means all. Here and at this present moment he is on his way towards the glory; and all the circumstances surrounding him are intended to help and not to hinder him, if only they are rightly understood. It is sadly true that in the world there is much of evil and of sorrow and of suffering; yet from the higher point of view the Theosophist sees that terrible though this be, it is only temporary and superficial, and is all being utilized as a factor in the progress.

When in the days of his ignorance he looked at it from its own level it was almost impossible to see this; while he looked from beneath at the under side of life, with his eyes fixed all the time upon some apparent evil, he could never gain a true grasp of its meaning. Now he raises himself above it to the higher levels of thought and consciousness, and looks down upon it with the eye of the spirit and understands it in its entirety, so he can see that in very truth all is well – not that all will be well at some remote period, but that even now at this moment, in the midst of incessant striving and apparent evil, the mighty current of evolution is still flowing, and so all is well because all is moving on in perfect order towards the final goal.

Raising his consciousness thus above the storm and stress of worldly life, he recognizes what used to seem to be evil, and notes how it is apparently pressing back-wards against the great stream of progress; but he also sees that the onward sweep of the divine law of evolution bears the same relation to this superficial evil as does the tremendous torrent of Niagara to the fleckings of foam upon its surface. So while he sympathizes deeply with all who suffer, he yet realizes what will be the end of that suffering, and so for him despair or hopelessness is impossible. He applies this consideration to his own sorrows and troubles, as well as to those of the world, and therefore one great result of his Theosophy is a perfect serenity – even more than that, a perpetual cheerfulness and joy.

For him there is an utter absence of worry, because in truth there is nothing left to worry about, since he knows that all must be well. His higher Science makes him a confirmed optimist, for it shows him that whatever of evil there may be in any person or in any movement, it is of necessity temporary, because it is opposed to the resistless stream of evolution; whereas whatever is good in any person or in any movement must necessarily be persistent and useful, because it has behind it the omnipotence of that current, and therefore it must abide and it must prevail.

Yet it must not for a moment be supposed that because he is so fully assured of the final triumph of good he remains careless or unmoved by the evils which exist in the world around him. He knows that it is his duty to combat these to the utmost of his power, because in doing this he is working upon the side of the great evolutionary force, and is bringing nearer the time of its ultimate victory. None will be more active than he in labouring for the good, even though he is absolutely free from the feeling of helplessness and hopelessness which so often oppresses those who are striving to help their fellowmen.

Another most valuable result of his Theosophical study is the absence of fear. Many people are constantly anxious or worried about something or other; they are fearing lest this or that should happen to them, lest this or that combination may fail, and so all the while they are in a condition of unrest; and most serious of all for many is the fear of death. For the Theosophist the whole of this feeling is entirely swept away. He realizes the great truth of reincarnation. He knows that he has often before laid aside physical bodies, and so he sees that death is no more than sleep – that just as sleep comes in between our days of work and gives us rest and refreshment, so between these days of labour here on earth, which we call lives, there comes a long night of astral and of heavenly life to give us rest and refreshment and to help us on our way.

To the Theosophist, death is simply the laying aside for a time of this robe of flesh. He knows that it is his duty to preserve the bodily vesture as long as possible, and gain through it all the experience he can; but when the time comes for him to lay it down he will do so thankfully, because he knows that the next stage will be a much pleasanter one than this. Thus he will have no fear of death, although he realizes that he must live his life to the appointed end, because he is here for the purpose of progress, and that progress is the one truly momentous matter. His whole conception of life is different; the object is not to earn so much money, not to obtain such and such a position; the one important thing is to carry out the divine plan. He knows that for this he is here, and that everything else must give way to it.

Utterly free also is he from any religious fears or worries or troubles. All such things are swept aside for him, because he sees clearly that progress towards the highest is the divine Will for us, that we cannot escape from that progress, and that whatever comes in our way and whatever happens to us is meant to help us along that line; that we ourselves are absolutely the only people who can delay our advance. No longer does he trouble and fear about himself. He simply goes on and does the duty which comes nearest in the best way that he can, confident that if he does this all will be well for him without his perpetual worrying. He is satisfied quietly to do his work and to try to help his fellows in the race, knowing that the great divine Power behind will press him onward slowly and steadily, and do for him all that can be done, so long as his face is set steadfastly in the right direction, so long as he does all that he reasonably can.

Since he knows that we are all part of one great evolution and all literally the children of one Father, he sees that the universal brotherhood of humanity is no mere poetical conception, but a definite fact; not a dream of something which is to be in the dim distance of Utopia, but a condition existing here and now. The certainty of this all-embracing fraternity gives him a wider outlook upon life and a broad impersonal point of view from which to regard everything. He realizes that the true interests of all are in fact identical, and that no man can ever make real gain for himself at the cost of loss or suffering to some one else. This is not to him an article of religious belief, but a scientific fact proved to him by his study. He sees that since humanity is literally a whole, nothing which injures one man can ever be really for the good of any other, for the harm done influences not only the doer but also those who are about him.

He knows that the only true advantage for him is that benefit which he shares with all. He sees that any advance which he is able to make in the way of spiritual progress or development is something secured not for himself alone but for others. If he gains knowledge or self-control, he assuredly acquires much for himself, yet he takes nothing away from anyone else, but on the contrary he helps and strengthens others. Cognizant as he is of the absolute spiritual unity of humanity, he knows that, even in this lower world, no true profit can be made by one man which is not made in the name of and for the sake of humanity; that one man's progress must be a lifting of the burden of all the others; that one man's advance in spiritual things means a very slight yet not imperceptible advance to humanity as a whole; that everyone who bears suffering and sorrow nobly in his struggle towards the light is lifting a little of the heavy load of the sorrow and suffering of his brothers as well.

Because he recognizes this brotherhood not merely as a hope cherished by despairing men, but as a definite fact following in scientific series from all other facts; because he sees this as an absolute certainty, his attitude towards all those around him changes radically. It becomes a posture ever of helpfulness, ever of the deepest sympathy, for he sees that nothing which clashes with their higher interests can be the right thing for him to do, or can be good for him in any way.

It naturally follows that he becomes filled with the widest possible tolerance and charity. He cannot but be always tolerant, because his philosophy shows him that it matters little what a man believes, so long as he is a good man and true. Charitable also he must be, because his wider knowledge enables him to make allowances for many things which the ordinary man does not understand. The standard of the Theosophist as to right and wrong is always higher than that of the less instructed man, yet he is far gentler than the latter in his feeling towards the sinner, because he comprehends more of human nature. He realizes how the sin appeared to the sinner at the moment of its commission, and so he makes more allowances than is ever made by the man who is ignorant of all this.

He goes further than tolerance, charity, sympathy; he feels positive love towards mankind, and that leads him to adopt a position of watchful helpfulness. He feels that every contact with others is for him an opportunity, and the additional knowledge which his study has brought to him enables him to give advice or help in almost any case which comes before him. Not that he is perpetually thrusting his opinions upon other people. On the contrary, he observes that to do this is one of the commonest mistakes made by the uninstructed. He knows that argument is a foolish waste of energy, and therefore he declines to argue. If anyone desires from him explanation or advice he is more than willing to give it, yet he has no sort of wish to convert anyone else to his own way of thinking.

In every relation of life this idea of helpfulness comes into play, not only with regard to his fellowmen but also in connection with the vast animal kingdom which surrounds him. Units of this kingdom are often brought into close relation with man, and this is for him an opportunity of doing something for them. The Theosophist recognizes that these are also his brothers, even though they may be younger brothers, and that he owes a fraternal duty to them also – so to act and so to think that his relation with them shall be always for their good and never for their harm.

Preeminently and above all, this Theosophy is to him a doctrine of common sense. It puts before him, as far as he can at present know them, the facts about God and man and the relations between them; then he proceeds to take these facts into account and to act in relation to them with ordinary reason and common sense. He regulates his life according to the laws of evolution which it has taught him, and this gives him a totally different standpoint, and a touchstone by which to try everything – his own thoughts and feelings, and his own actions first of all, and then those things which come before him in the world outside himself.

Always he applies this criterion: Is the thing right or wrong, does it help evolution or does it hinder it? If a thought or a feeling arises within himself, he sees at once by this test whether it is one he ought to encourage. If it be for the greatest good of the greatest number then all is well; if it may hinder or cause harm to any being in its progress, then it is evil and to be avoided. Exactly the same reason holds good if he is called upon to decide with regard to anything outside himself. If from that point of view a thing be a good thing, then he can conscientiously support it; if not, then it is not for him.

For him the question of personal interest does not come into the case at all. He thinks simply of the good of evolution as a whole. This gives him a definite foothold and the clear criterion, and removes from him altogether the pain of indecision and hesitation. The Will of the Deity is man's evolution; whatever therefore helps on that evolution must be good; whatever stands in the way of it and delays it, that thing must be wrong, even though it may have on its side all the weight of public opinion and immemorial tradition.

Knowing that the true man is the ego and not the body, he sees that it is the life of the ego only which is really of moment, and that everything connected with the body must unhesitatingly be subordinated to those higher interests. He recognizes that this earth-life is given to him for the purpose of progress, and that that progress is the one important thing. The real purpose of his life is the unfoldment of his powers as an ego, the development of his character. He knows that there must be evolvement not only of the physical body but also of the mental nature, of the mind and of the spiritual perceptions. He sees that nothing short of absolute perfection is expected of him in connection with this development; that all power with regard to it is in his own hands; that he has everlasting time before him in which to attain this perfection, but that the sooner it is gained the happier and more useful will he be.

He recognizes his life as nothing but a day at school, and his physical body as a temporary vesture assumed for the purpose of learning through it. He knows at once that this purpose of learning lessons is the only one of any real importance, and that the man who allows himself to be diverted from that purpose by any consideration whatever is acting with inconceivable stupidity. To him, the life devoted exclusively to physical objects, to the acquisition of wealth or fame, appears the merest child's play – a senseless sacrifice of all that is really worth having for the sake of a few moments' gratification of the lower part of his nature. He "sets his affection on things above and not on things of the earth", not only because he sees this to be the right course of action, but because he realizes so clearly the valuelessness of these things of earth. He always tries to take the higher point of view, for he knows that the lower is utterly unreliable – that the lower desires and feelings gather round him like a dense fog, and make it impossible for him to see anything clearly from that level.

Whenever he finds a struggle going on within him he remembers that he himself is the higher, and that this which is the lower is not the real self, but merely an uncontrolled part of one of its vehicles. He knows that though he may fall a thousand times on the way towards his goal, his reason for trying to reach it remains just as strong after the thousandth fall as it was in the beginning, so that it would not only be useless but unwise and wrong to give way to despondency and hopelessness.

He begins his journey upon the road of progress at once – not only because he knows that it is far easier for him now than it will be if he leaves the effort until later, but chiefly because if he makes the endeavour now and succeeds in achieving some progress, if he rises thereby to some higher level, he is in a position to hold out a helping hand to those who have not yet reached even that step on the ladder which he has gained. In that way he takes a part, however humble it may be, in the great divine work of evolution.

He knows that he has arrived at his present position only by a slow process of growth, and so he does not expect instantaneous attainment of perfection. He sees how inevitable is the great law of cause and effect, and that when he once grasps the working of that law he can use it intelligently in regard to mental and moral development, just as in the physical world we can employ for our own assistance those laws of Nature the action of which we have learnt to understand.

Understanding what death is, he knows that there can be no need to fear it or to mourn over it, whether it comes to himself or to those whom he loves. It has come to them all often before, so there is nothing unfamiliar about it. He sees death simply as a promotion from a life which is more than half physical to one which is wholly superior, so for himself he unfeignedly welcomes it; and even when it comes to those whom he loves, he recognizes at once the advantage for them, even though he cannot but feel a pang of regret that he should be temporarily separated from them so far as the physical world is concerned. But he knows that the so-called dead are near him still, and that he has only to cast off for a time his physical body in sleep in order to stand side by side with them as before.

He sees clearly that the world is one, and that the same divine laws rule the whole of it, whether it be visible or invisible to physical sight. So he has no feeling of nervousness or strangeness in passing from one part of it to another, and no feeling of uncertainty as to what he will find on the other side of the veil. He knows that in that higher life there opens before him a splendid vista of opportunities both for acquiring fresh knowledge and for doing useful work; that life away from this dense body has a vividness and a brilliancy to which all earthly enjoyment is as nothing; and so through his clear knowledge and calm confidence the power of the endless life shines out upon all those round him.

Doubt as to his future is for him impossible, for just as by looking back on the savage he realizes that which he was in the past, so by looking to the greatest and wisest of mankind he knows what he will be in the future. He sees an unbroken chain of development, a ladder of perfection rising steadily before him, yet with human beings upon every step of it, so that he knows that those steps are possible for him to climb. It is just because of the unchangeableness of the great law of cause and effect that he finds himself able to climb that ladder, because since the law works always in the same way, he can depend upon it and he can use it, just as he uses the laws of Nature in the physical worlds. His knowledge of this law brings to him a sense of perspective and shows him that if something comes to him, it comes because he has deserved it as a consequence of actions which he has committed, of words which he has spoken, of thought to which he has given harbour in previous days or in earlier lives. He comprehends that all affliction is of the nature of the payment of a debt, and therefore when he has to meet with the troubles of life he takes them and uses them as a lesson, because he understands why they have come and is glad of the opportunity which they give him to pay off something of his obligation.

Again, and in yet another way, does he take them as an opportunity, for he sees that there is another side to them if he meets them in the right way. He spends no time in bearing prospective burdens. When trouble comes to him he does not aggravate it by foolish repining but sets himself to endure so much of it as is inevitable, with patience and with fortitude. Not that he submits himself to it as a fatalist might, for he takes adverse circumstances as an incentive to such development as may enable him to transcend them, and thus out of long-past evil he brings forth a seed of future growth. For in the very act of paying the outstanding debt he develops qualities of courage and resolution that will stand him in good stead through all the ages that are to come.

He is distinguishable from the rest of the world by his perennial cheerfulness, his undaunted courage under difficulties, and his ready sympathy and helpfulness; yet he is at the same time emphatically a man who takes life seriously, who recognizes that there is much for everyone to do in the world, and that there is no time to waste. He knows with utter certainty that he not only makes his own destiny but also gravely affects that of others around him, and thus he perceives how weighty a responsibility attends the use of his power.

He knows that thoughts are things and that it is easily possible to do great harm or great good by their means, He knows that no man liveth to himself, for his every thought acts upon others as well; that the vibrations which he sends forth from his mind and from his mental nature are reproducing themselves in the minds and the mental natures of other men, so that he is a source either of mental health or of mental ill to all with whom he comes in contact.

This at once imposes upon him a far higher code of social ethics than that which is known to the outer world, for he knows that he must control not only his acts and his words, but also his thoughts, since they may produce effects more serious and more far-reaching than their outward expression in the physical world. He knows that even when a man is not in the least thinking of others, he yet inevitably affects them for good or for evil. In addition to this unconscious action of his thought upon others he also employs it consciously for good. He sets currents in motion to carry mental help and comfort to many a suffering friend, and in this way he finds a whole new world of usefulness opening before him.

He ranges himself ever on the side of the higher rather than the lower thought, the nobler rather than the baser. He deliberately takes the optimistic rather than the pessimistic view of everything, the helpful, rather than the cynical, because he knows that to be fundamentally the true view. By looking continually for the good in everything that he may endeavour to strengthen it, by striving always to help and never to hinder, he becomes ever of greater use to his fellowmen, and is thus in his small way a co-worker with the splendid scheme of evolution. He forgets himself utterly and lives but for the sake of others, realizing himself as a part of that scheme; he also realizes the God within him, and learns to become ever a truer expression of Him, and thus in fulfilling God's Will, he is not only blessed himself, but becomes a blessing to all.

Other Books by C.W. LEADBEATER published by AZILOTH BOOKS

The Astral Plane – its scenery, inhabitants and phenomena
(First published 1895)

C. W. Leadbeater was one of the foremost writers on theosophical topics in the early 20th century. He is the father of neo-theosophy, a man credited with great occult ability, whose prolific writings cover a wide range of esoteric topics, from descriptions of the super-physical worlds, through humanity's occult past and potential future, to the remote-viewing of atoms and sub-atomic particles.

In *The Astral Plane* he focuses on the plane of existence which lies just above our own, and which we visit during periods of lucid dreaming. Leadbeater's account describes the astral's environment and spiritual denizens in great detail: here we find descriptions of angels, elementals, fairies, vampires, werewolves and black magicians, and explanations for psychic phenomena such as clairvoyance, levitation, churchyard ghosts, spirit photographs and mysterious bell-ringing. Written in Leadbeater's eloquent, matter-of-fact style, *The Astral Plane* is one of the best introductions to this otherworldly realm.

The Devachanic Plane: the Heaven World and its Inhabitants
(First published 1896)

Charles Webster Leadbeater was an ordained Anglican priest who left his Church to follow the spiritual disciplines and teachings of the Theosophical Society. In 1883 he traveled to India and underwent strict spiritual training, including kundalini yoga, a discipline that vivifies the chakras and opens the third eye.

Leadbeater endeavoured to communicate these spiritual revelations to the general public in a series of books, of which *The Devachanic Plane* remains an enduring classic. The work describes all aspects of devachan - the astral 'heaven world' - its characteristics, its language, and the human, non-human and artificial inhabitants that exist there. Essential reading for all students of the occult.

Thought-Forms (with Annie Besant)
(First published 1901)

In this, one of the few colour editions of *Thought-Forms*, Annie Besant describes how the human aura changes constantly in size, form and colour, depending an individual's mental and emotional state. The book features the original fifty-eight colour illustrations that give the reader a direct experience of a psychic's impressions of the aura, what Besant herself called "the living light of other worlds". For Besant and her followers, thoughts were as real and powerful as words or deeds, her hope being that the vibrant images would allow everyone to "realise the nature and power of his thoughts, acting as a stimulus to the noble, a curb on the base".

Born in London on 1st October 1847, Annie Besant was described as a 'diamond soul', a complex mix of spiritual seeker and social reformer, advocating progressive ideas on such topics as education, trade unions, birth control, female suffrage and Irish and Indian self-rule. Besant eventually settled in the sub-continent, embraced theosophy, and wrote widely on the religious movement's views on karma, reincarnation and the purpose of human existence. She was herself blessed with spiritual gifts, one of which – the ability to view an individual's aura or psychic energy field – forms the basis of this present work.

Charles W. Leadbeater was ordained as an Anglican priest but gradually felt drawn towards gnosticism and theosophy. He met Annie Besant in 1894, a few years after she became president of the Theosophical Society, and collaborated with her in exploring such shared interests as the human aura, aspects of the soul and occult chemistry.

The Inner Life – Vols. I & II
(First published 1911)

Vol. I – Charles Webster Leadbeater is regarded as one of the most important of the twentieth century's writers on theosophy. A competent seer and teacher, the series of lectures which comprise Volumes I and II were given to students in the early 1900s, during evening 'talks' at the Theosophical Society's headquarters at Adyar in India.

The Inner Life: Volume I gives the theosophical perspective on a vast swathe of esoteric subjects, from Ascended Masters to the devil, and from the world's major religions through kundalini and meditation to our duty to animals. Leadbeater's descriptions expand and elaborate on the ancient tradition that has been an occult heritage of humankind since before the dawn of history – much of which is now being verified by scientific data from both quantum- and bio-physics.

A fascinating compendium of esoteric knowledge that no student of the occult should be without.

Vol. II – *The Inner Life* considers a wide range of topics, from life after death to nature spirits, and from reincarnation through psychic powers to work on the astral plane. As in Volume I, Leadbeater's descriptions in Volume II expand and elaborate on the ancient tradition that has been mankind's age-old heritage.

The Hidden Side of Things – Vols. I & II
(First published 1913)

Charles Webster Leadbeater was inducted into the Theosophical Society in

London on November 21, 1883. A year later he left for India with Madame H. P. Blavatsky, where he underwent training in several spiritual disciplines, including kundalini yoga, which purports to both vivify the chakras and open the third eye.

The revelations he received were channeled into over a score of books, all designed to make spiritual teachings more easily understood by the general public. *The Hidden Side of Things* is among the best of these works, describing the array of energies that an individual both emanates, and also receives from a vast range of sources. Filled with astounding detail, this book will change the way you look at the world. It is essential reading for students of the occult and, indeed, for anyone wishing to understand humanity's place in the spiritual realms.

The Masters and the Path
(First published 1925)

Charles Webster Leadbeater was ordained an Anglian priest in 1879 but, just four years later, a deep interest in spiritualism and the occult caused him to sever his ties with the church and to join the Theosophical Society, where he soon became a high official.

Leadbeater traveled extensively in India and described meeting and training under Ascended Masters who, (according to Madame Blavatsky), were the secret chiefs of the theosophical movement. One important result of this experience was his classic occult manual *The Masters and the Path*, which explores the route of discipleship under the guidance of Ascended Masters. An inspiring and uplifting work, eloquently written, it reveals innumerable details concerning the way of the masters, exploration of the inner planes, the disciplines required for advancement, and the plans gradually being put in place by these advanced beings for the unfolding of human consciousness.

AZILOTH BOOKS

Aziloth Books publishes a wide range of titles ranging from hard-to-find esoteric books - *Parehment Books* - to classic works on fiction, politics and philosophy - *Cathedral Classics*. Our newest venture is *Aziloth Books Children's Classics*, with vibrant new covers and illustrations to complement some of the world's very best children's tales. All our imprints are offered to the reader at a competitive price and through as many mediums and outlets as possible.

We are committed to excellent book production and strive, whenever possible, to add value to our titles with original images, maps and author introductions. With the premium on space in most modern dwellings, we also endeavour - within the limits of good book design - to make our products as slender as possible, allowing more books to be fitted into a given bookshelf area.

We are a small, approachable company and would love to hear any of your comments and suggestions on our plans, products, or indeed on absolutely anything.

Aziloth Books, Rimey Law, Rookhope, Co. Durham, DL13 2BL, England.
t: 01388-517600 e: info@azilothbooks.com w: www.azilothbooks.com

Parchment Books enshrines the concept of the oneness of all true religious traditions - that "the light shines from many different lanterns". Our list below offers titles from both eastern and western spiritual traditions, including Christian, Judaic, Islamic, Daoist, Hindu and Buddhist mystical texts, as well as books on alchemy, hermeticism, paganism, etc..

By bringing together such spiritual texts, we hope to make esoteric and occult knowledge more readily available to those ready to receive it. We do not publish grimoires or any titles pertaining to the left hand path. Titles include:

Abandonment to Divine Providence	Jean-Pierre de Caussade
Corpus Hermeticum	G. R. S. Mead (trans.)
The Holy Rule of St Benedict	St. Benedict of Nursia
The Way of Perfection	St. Teresa of Avila
The Cloud Upon the Sanctuary	Karl von Eckhartshausen
The Confession of St Patrick	St. Patrick
The Outline of Sanity	G. K. Chesterton
The Dialogue Of St Catherine Of Siena	St. Catherine of Siena
Esoteric Christianity	Annie Besant
The Spiritual Exercises of St. Ignatius	St. Ignatius of Loyola
Dark Night of the Soul	St. John of the Cross
The Gospel of Thomas	Anonymous
St. Francis	G. K. Chesterton
The Imitation of Christ	Thomas à Kempis
The Interior Castle	St. Teresa of Avila
Songs of Innocence & Experience	William Blake
The Marriage of Heaven & Hell	William Blake
The Secret of the Rosary	St. Louis Marie de Montfort
From Ritual to Romance	Jessie L. Weston
The God of the Witches	Margaret Murray

Obtainable at all good online and local bookstores.
View Aziloth Books' full list at: www.azilothbooks.com

Cathedral Classics hosts an array of classic literature, from erudite ancient tomes to avant-garde, twentieth-century masterpieces, all of which deserve a place in your home. All the world's great novelists are here, Jane Austen, Dickens, Conrad, Arthur Machen and Henry James, brushing shoulders with such disparate luminaries as Sun Tzu, Marcus Aurelius, Kipling, Friedrich Nietzsche, Machiavelli, and Omar Khayam. A small selection is detailed below:

The Prophet	Kahlil Gibran
Herland	Charlotte Perkins Gilman
With Her in Ourland	Charlotte Perkins Gilman
Frankenstein	Mary Shelley
The Time Machine; The Invisible Man	H. G. Wells
Three Men in a Boat	Jerome K Jerome
The Rubaiyat of Omar Khayyam	Omar Khayyam
A Study in Scarlet	Arthur Conan Doyle
Persuasion	Jane Austen
The Picture of Dorian Gray	Oscar Wilde
Flatland	Edwin A. Abbott
The Coming Race	Bulwer Lytton
The Adventures of Sherlock Holmes	Arthur Conan Doyle
The Great God Pan	Arthur Machen
Beyond Good and Evil	Friedrich Nietzsche
England, My England	D. H. Lawrence
The Castle of Otranto	Horace Walpole
Self-Reliance, & Other Essays (series1&2)	Ralph W. Emmerson
The Art of War	Sun Tzu
A Shepherd's Life	W. H. Hudson
The Double	Fyodor Dostoyevsky
To the Lighthouse; Mrs. Dalloway	Virginia Woolf
The Sorrows of Young Werther	Johann W. Goethe
Leaves of Grass - 1855 edition	Walt Whitman
Analects	Confucius
Beowulf	Anonymous
Agnes Grey	Anne Bronte
Plain Tales From The Hills	Rudyard Kipling
The Subjection of Women	John Stuart Mill
Silas Marner	George Eliot
The Rights of Man	Thomas Paine
Herland	Charlotte Perkins Gilman

Obtainable at all good online and local bookstores.
View Aziloth Books' full list at: www.azilothbooks.com

Aziloth Books is passionate about bringing the very best in children's classics fiction to the next generation of book-lovers. Renowned for its original design and outstanding quality, our highly successful list has something to suit every age and interest. Titles include:

The Railway Children	Edith Nesbit
5 Children and It	Edith Nesbit
Anne of Green Gables	Lucy Maud Montgomery
What Katy Did	Susan Coolidge
What Katy Did Next	Susan Coolidge
Puck of Pook's Hill	Rudyard Kipling
The Jungle Books	Rudyard Kipling
Just So Stories	Rudyard Kipling
Alice Through the Looking Glass	Charles Dodgson
Alice's Adventures in Wonderland	Charles Dodgson
Black Beauty	Anna Sewell
The War of the Worlds	H. G Wells
The Time Machine	H. G .Wells
The Sleeper Awakes	H. G. Wells
The Invisible Man	H. G. Wells
The Lost World	Sir Arthur Conan Doyle
A Christmas Carol	Charles Dickens
Call of the Wild	Jack London
Greenmantle	John Buchan
Treasure Island	Robert Louis Stevenson
Dr Jekyll and Mr. Hyde	Robert Louis Stevenson
Gulliver's Travels	Jonathan Swift
Catriona (David Balfour)	Robert Louis Stevenson
The Water Babies	Charles Kingsley
The First Men in the Moon	Jules Verne
The Secret Garden	Frances Hodgson Burnett
A Little Princess	Frances Hodgson Burnett
Peter Pan	J. M. Barrie
The Song of Hiawatha	Henry W. Longfellow

Obtainable at all good online and local bookstores.
View Aziloth Books' full list at: www.azilothbooks.com

www.ingramcontent.com/pod-product-compliance
Lightning Source LLC
Chambersburg PA
CBHW071321040426
42444CB00009B/2063